D0095153

Harper Lee

UP *close:*

Harper Lee

a twentieth-century life by
KERRY MADDEN

VIKING

VIKING

Published by Penguin Group

Penguin Young Readers Group, 345 Hudson Street, New York, New York 10014, U.S.A.

Penguin Group (Canada), 90 Eglinton Avenue East, Suite 700, Toronto, Ontario,
Canada M4P 2Y3 (a division of Pearson Penguin Canada Inc.)

Penguin Books Ltd, 80 Strand, London WC2R 0RL, England

Penguin Ireland, 25 St Stephen's Green, Dublin 2, Ireland (a division of Penguin Books Ltd)

Penguin Group (Australia), 250 Camberwell Road, Camberwell, Victoria 3124, Australia
(a division of Pearson Australia Group Pty Ltd)

Penguin Books India Pvt Ltd, 11 Community Centre, Panchsheel Park, New Delhi – 110 017, India

Penguin Group (NZ), 67 Apollo Drive, Rosedale, North Shore 0632, New Zealand
(a division of Pearson New Zealand Ltd)

Penguin Books (South Africa) (Pty) Ltd, 24 Sturdee Avenue, Rosebank, Johannesburg 2196,
South Africa

Penguin Books Ltd, Registered Offices: 80 Strand, London WC2R 0RL, England

First published in 2009 by Viking, a division of Penguin Young Readers Group

10 9 8 7 6 5 4 3 2

LIBRARY OF CONGRESS CATALOGING-IN-PUBLICATION DATA
Madden, Kerry.
Harper Lee / Kerry Madden.
p. cm. — (Up close)
Includes bibliographical references and index.
ISBN 978-0-670-01095-0
1. Lee, Harper—Juvenile literature. 2. Authors, American—
20th century—Biography—Juvenile literature. I. Title.
PS3562.E353Z76 2009
813'.54—dc22
[B]
2008053911

Printed in the U.S.A.
Set in Goudy
Book design by Jim Hoover

For my sister, Keely, who fills my
life with stories and laughter

Contents

Harper Lee

My needs are simple: paper, pen, and privacy.
—HARPER LEE

Foreword

WHEN I WAS asked to write a young adult biography of Harper Lee for Viking's Up Close Series, I set out on the task of trying to contact her through her agent in New York and her oldest sister in Alabama. A colleague of mine who had recently met her sent a letter of introduction to her on my behalf. I also wrote at least ten drafts of my own letter to Miss Lee. It's a daunting task to write to such a beloved and passionately silent author, who has been known to respond "Hell no!" to interview requests. But I needed to make sure that Miss Lee knew about the biography before anybody else did. I wanted to tread with care and respect every step of the way.

When her reply came, it was short and succinct. She does not believe in biographies for those still living. She wrote, "I may be old but I'm still breathing." She closed the note wishing me the best, whether I pursued the project or not. It was disappointing, but certainly not unexpected. She hasn't granted an interview to discuss her work since 1964, and has even turned down Oprah. I thanked her and decided to continue with the book anyway. Harper Lee's was a story I longed to write.

I grew up in football towns across the South and Midwest. My father was a college coach in search of the opportunity to win, so we picked up and moved often. Alabama football legend Bear Bryant was one of our family's patron saints. With each move, I searched for a sense of home, and I found it in books. One of my most cherished books was *To Kill a Mockingbird*. The first time I saw the film was on the big screen at the Tennessee Theatre in downtown Knoxville. Each time I reread the book or show my own children the film, I find home all over again. I can roam the streets of Harper Lee's "Maycomb" and hear the voices of Jem and Scout and Dill calling to one another. I had a cousin just like sniveling cousin Francis. I beat up a boy like Cecil Jacobs.

My father even advised me to attend the University of Alabama, Harper Lee's alma mater, in order to join the women's golf team, since I played on the boys' team in high school. But I loved books and wanted to be an exchange student in England, so I didn't play golf in college. Though I did study in England for a year at Manchester University.

Harper Lee wrote in *To Kill a Mockingbird*: "Real courage is when you know you're licked, before you begin, but you begin anyway and see it through no matter what." The more I began to work on her biography, the more those words began to haunt me. I realized I might very well be licked, with my subject not willing to talk and so little published about her—except for one unauthorized biography. So to find real courage to write this book, I knew I needed to go to the heart of Harper Lee country. I wanted an understanding not just of the author but also of her home and the people who know her. It was the only way I knew how to write the story.

So in the spring of 2007, I attended the Alabama Book Festival in Montgomery, and then took 1-65 south to Highway 84 West, eventually arriving in

Monroeville. My sister, Keely, came with me on the first trip to help with all the interviews and research. We went to the Old Courthouse Museum to research the archives and study newspaper clippings, press releases, and photographs. I made two more trips to Monroeville during the course of writing the book, for additional interviews, research, and school visits to do writing workshops with students as part of Alabama Voices.

On one of my research trips to Alabama, I took my nine-year-old daughter, Norah, and we arrived in Monroeville on an early Sunday evening in February. The old clock tower struck five on the town square while she raced around, gathering pink, red, and white camellias that had fallen on the grass. With her arms full of flowers, she stopped and said, "This place is beautiful but it's lonesome and sad too."

I came to think of Harper Lee as "Nelle" (pronounced "nail" in Monroeville), so in this book I refer to her as Nelle and occasionally Harper. As a girl, she hated it when people mispronounced her name "Nellie," which was why she later chose to use her middle name, "Harper," when *To Kill a Mockingbird* was published.

Many people refused to speak to me out of respect for Nelle's privacy, but others did want to share their stories. We found classmates, colleagues, and even Miss Lee's older sister, Miss Alice Finch Lee, age ninety-seven, whom we disturbed at work where she was reading a law brief. Alice Lee is one of the oldest working attorneys in the United States, and she still goes to the office three days a week. She calls her sister "Nelle Harper," and she kindly declined to grant us an interview.

All week long, Keely and I walked the streets of Monroeville and drove the back roads along the Alabama River. In his book *Alabama on My Mind*, Wayne Greenhaw describes Alabama as "a beautiful, remarkable, complex country. . . . Such names as Murder Creek, Burnt Corn community, Fort Mims massacre, Chief Red Eagle of the Creeks peppered conversations. The land was scarred with human tragedy."

At the Old Courthouse, we climbed the worn painted brown pine staircase to the oval-shaped courtroom, an exact replica of which was built for Atticus Finch to defend Tom Robinson in the movie version of *To Kill a Mockingbird*. We listened to the museum curator, Jane Ellen Clark, describe how some visitors walk inside and break down crying because of powerful memories evoked by the book and film.

The back-to-back interviews with the people of Monroeville lasted eight to ten hours a day, and what we came away with was a sense of Nelle Harper Lee as very much a regular person. She loves to fish and listen to gospel music in the little churches on the back roads of Alabama. She hates eggs, which was why she always skipped breakfast while a college student at the University of Alabama in the 1940s. She has great sea legs and enjoyed gourmet meals in the middle of a thunderstorm while sailing from England on the *QE2* in the 1960s. She once waited for friends to meet her at the Russian Tea Room in New York City, sipping a martini and reading Eudora Welty. The evening later inspired a poem by Alabama author Wayne Greenhaw that begins, "Miss Lee and I go dancing." She adores young people and will always take the time to talk to them and listen to their stories or answer their questions.

A clerk at the Monroeville Post Office said five or six fan letters still typically arrive every week, usually from adults, and Nelle picks them up herself if she's in town. She spends roughly half the year in Alabama and the other half in New York, although lately she has spent more time in Alabama because of health issues and to be closer to her sister. All over town, folks described seeing Nelle Harper in jeans and T-shirts at Hardee's, McDonald's, the Huddle House, and David's Catfish. But the librarian of Monroeville, Bunny Hines, explained Nelle best when she described a lady from up north who came in and desperately wanted to send Harper Lee a bouquet of flowers. "She was so sweet, bless her heart, but I had to discourage the woman. Nelle doesn't want flowers and fancy gifts sent to her. Nelle is just plain folks."

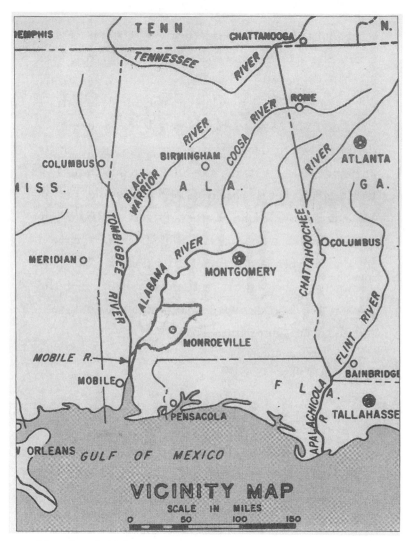

Map of south Alabama.

Introduction

NELLE HARPER LEE "comes from a generation of writers who never appeared on *Oprah*, people who were fairly private. And as we've made stars and personalities of our novelists, we can't understand why anybody would want to keep their private lives private. Everybody wants to be on TV."

—Professor Claudia Durst Johnson, a Harper Lee scholar and former University of Alabama English Department chairman.

The last thing Harper Lee would ever want is to be on television, or anywhere near the spotlight. She was never comfortable being the center of attention, which is where she was thrust almost immediately upon the publication of her first and only novel. She was utterly unprepared for the onslaught of publicity and interview requests that poured in, and tried to reply promptly and directly to each one, at least in the beginning.

In a brief response to a request from her alma mater, Huntingdon College, she wrote: "I'm afraid a biographical sketch of me will be sketchy indeed; with the exception of M'Bird, nothing of any particular interest to anyone has happened to me in my thirty-four years." She went on to describe her education in the Monroeville schools, Huntingdon College, and the University of Alabama, explaining that if she had ever learned anything she'd forgotten it. She said her writing day began at noon and ended at midnight with a dinner break. Her idea of "play" was "reading, golf, and going through secondhand bookstores." She closed her letter by saying she couldn't think of anything else to share.

It's possible that Alice had encouraged Nelle to answer Huntingdon's request quickly, since by that time Alice was handling all of her younger sister's *To Kill a Mockingbird*–related affairs. Neither of them believed the arrangement would be permanent. They didn't think the book's tremendous success could last.

OVERVIEW OF
To Kill a Mockingbird

IT MUST HAVE seemed to Nelle that there were rules for everything while she was growing up in Monroeville. How to chew your food—slowly please! How to stand—don't slouch! How to enter a room—walk, don't run. Rules on top of rules! Girls couldn't deliver the newspaper. Children answered their elders with "Yes, ma'am" or "no, ma'am" or "No, sir" or "yes, sir," and never addressed a teacher by a first name. Everybody belonged to a church, either Baptist or Methodist. Whistling at the dinner table was forbidden and exhibited the worst kind of manners.

In the only book she ever published, Nelle captured her own life in a small Southern town and made it into something universal. Told through the eyes of a child, *To Kill a Mockingbird* is the story of Scout Finch growing up in the fictionalized town of Maycomb in the 1930s, during the Great Depression. Scout's brother, Jem, is her constant companion, and their best friend is Dill, a boy who lives next door with his aunt Stephanie during the summers. Scout, Jem, and Dill play together, acting out dramas and games from books they've read until they finally turn their attention to a ramshackle house where a recluse, or "haint," named Boo Radley lives. Neighborhood legend says that he is more than six feet tall, eats raw squirrels, and roams the streets at night.

Atticus Finch, the father of Scout and Jem, is one of the most beloved characters in American literature. He is a lawyer, assigned to defend a black man, Tom Robinson, who is accused of raping a white woman, Mayella Ewell. Scout and Jem endure vicious taunts and ridicule from both peers and adults in the town because of their father's decision to take the case and defend his client. The evidence is overwhelming that Tom Robinson could not have committed the crime, but the all-white jury finds him guilty and sentences him to death. During this period in the South, no jury would ever believe the word of a black man over a white man or woman. Although Atticus intends to appeal the verdict, Tom attempts to run away and is shot and killed by a prison guard. Mayella Ewell's father, Bob Ewell, remains so outraged by Atticus's belief in Tom Robinson's word over his own that he seeks revenge and sets out to kill Scout and Jem one night after the trial. It is Boo Radley, the boogeyman, who comes to their rescue.

The character of Dill in *To Kill a Mockingbird* was inspired by Nelle's friendship with another writer, Truman Capote, who lived next door to her when they were children. Truman was different, and the two of them naturally gravitated toward each other. Truman craved books and stories, much like Nelle herself. He even put her in his first novel, *Other Rooms, Other Voices,* as the character Idabel Tompkins. And he eventually encouraged Nelle to move to New York to write. Truman became a very famous author, too, writing *Breakfast at Tiffany's, In Cold Blood,* and *Music for Chameleons.*

❋ ❋ ❋

Today, a signed first edition of *To Kill a Mockingbird* is estimated to be worth more than $20,000. The novel has sold over thirty million copies in forty languages, and it continues to sell over ten thousand copies a year. High school teachers assign it more than almost any other novel, which means that, like William Shakespeare, Nathaniel Hawthorne, and Mark Twain, Harper Lee is one of the authors most read by American students.

Another Southern writer, Flannery O'Connor, said, "Anybody who has survived his childhood has enough information about life to last him the rest of his days." This was certainly true for Nelle, whose novel had autobiographical roots. Unlike Scout's family, Nelle's immediate family included a father, mother, two sisters, and a brother. Yet the book captures the "clime and tone" of her childhood in Monroeville, where she watched her father, a lawyer, "argue cases and talk to juries."

In the thirty-fifth-anniversary printing of *To Kill a Mockingbird* in February 1993, Nelle wrote an introduction explaining that she didn't like introductions and that "Mockingbird" had survived all these years without "preamble." Everything she had to say was already in the book. Her position has not changed in almost five decades, and she has steadfastly reminded reporters that if they want to know her they should simply read the book.

Chapter One

NELLE HARPER LEE was a kid who stomped through flower beds, shot rubber-band guns, and once broke a boy's front tooth. She even mopped the pavement with "Big Boy," whose real name was Jennings Carter. It made his mama so mad she could have beat Nelle's bottom off, and she said so.

Even playing games, Nelle could be rough. As "queen of the tomboys," Nelle raced around on the playground in a fierce battle of dodgeball one day at school. During the game, a boy kept sneaking up behind her to yank her hair. The first two times, he was successful, but by the third time, she was ready for him and punched him in the stomach. Humiliated, the boy sought the help of two boys to get even, but when Nelle quickly beat up his friends, one right after the other, all three took off running.

Street Scene, looking South, Monroeville, Ala.

South Alabama Avenue, the street where Nelle grew up, 1915. A car is parked in front of the Lee home.

Once when Nelle was up to bat during the girls' physical recreation period, Jane Hybart was playing first base. The shortstop intercepted Nelle's grounder and threw it toward first base. Instead of letting herself be thrown out, Nelle plowed right over the first baseman, knocking her flat.

"Like a freight train," Jane Hybart Rosborough recalled some seventy years later.

Nelle was born on April 28, 1926, in Monroeville, Alabama, the youngest of four children. She lived on South Alabama Avenue about a block from the town square, in a white house with a front porch swing, which was perfect for rocking on warm summer nights. She grew up with the nickname "Dody." It may have felt to Nelle like she had been born into a family of grown-ups. Her oldest sister, Alice, or "Bear" as she was called, was fifteen years her senior and close to going off to college in Montgomery by the time Nelle was born. Louise ("Weezie") was ten years older than Nelle and considered the prettiest girl in the Lee family. But Weezie was too busy with her studies and friends to have much time to play with her youngest sibling. Nelle's brother, Edwin, whom they called "Brother," was six years older, and was one of Nelle's first storytellers.

Perhaps the most influential person in Nelle's life was her father, Amasa Coleman Lee. He was the kind of father who encouraged all of his children to become educated and to work hard in any career they chose. This made him something of an anomaly in the South, where traditionally daughters were expected to be ladylike in all manner of dress and activities. If girls attended the University of Alabama at all, it was often primarily to find a husband. But Mr. Lee never seemed to burden any of his daughters with the expectation of marriage and motherhood. By his own example, he instilled in them

Amasa "A.C." Coleman Lee, 1961.   *Frances Finch Lee (date unknown).*

the value of contributing to society in positive ways.

A. C. Lee was born in Alabama in 1880 and moved with his family to Florida when he was two. He started off as a teacher in Florida at the age of sixteen but wanted a better job, so he moved to Monroe County to work as a bookkeeper for the Bear Creek Mill Company in Manistee, Alabama. When the company went under in 1905, he worked at another sawmill in North Monroe County. Nelle's mother, Frances Finch Cunningham Lee, was born in North Monroe County,

Alabama, in 1888 and lived on a plantation with 9,000 acres. Mr. Lee eventually met his future wife in Finchburg, Alabama.

After Nelle's parents married on June 22, 1910, they lived in Florida, where Alice was born in 1911. Louise arrived in 1916, followed by Edwin in 1920. Six years later, Nelle was born. Her name was Ellen spelled backward, after her maternal grandmother.

In 1913, the law firm Barnett and Bugg hired Mr. Lee to move to Monroeville to manage a railroad the firm owned. He was also a self-taught lawyer and became a member of the Alabama State Legislature. In those days, ambitious young men could become lawyers by studying and reading law books on their own. They did not have to attend law school. Mr. Lee passed the Alabama State bar exam in 1915.

After he became a lawyer, the law firm changed its name to Barnett, Bugg & Lee. While still practicing law, Mr. Lee became the editor of the local town newspaper, the *Monroe Journal*, and was editor from 1928 to 1947. In his editorials, Mr. Lee took the time to explain situations in clear and simple language. People in town admired and respected him as a voice of reason.

When Nelle's mother had insomnia, she'd play the

piano deep into the night. The crystal clear notes drift-ed out the open windows of the Lee home and could sometimes be heard all the way up to the town square.

Mrs. Lee was overweight and had what her daugh-ter Alice described as a "nervous disorder," which some people say may have been due to depression or possibly bipolar disorder, when a person's moods swing from the highest of highs to the lowest of lows. Sometimes Mrs. Lee talked a blue streak to passersby, while at other times she'd retreat into silence. Nelle's friend Truman claimed that in one of her more ver-bose states, Mrs. Lee inspired the first short story he wrote as a child, called "Mrs. Busybody." Another lady said Mrs. Lee used to call out to her from the front porch, "Get out of the hot sun!" whenever she'd pass by the house on her way to work.

The neighborhood paperboy, A. B. Blass, described Mrs. Lee as a quiet lady who sat on the porch swing each day almost as if in a private dreamworld. When he arrived on his bicycle, Mrs. Lee would always repeat the same thing in a gentle voice: "You're certainly a nice young man."

Mr. Lee took his wife out for drives, and a resi-dent who remembered seeing them on a regular basis described Mrs. Lee as seated in the front seat, staring straight ahead, never waving or making eye contact. In the South, it is a common practice to wave to friends and strangers as a form of polite greeting, but often Mrs. Lee did not. People who recalled Nelle's mother remember her as a distant woman. But in a letter published in O magazine, Nelle said her mother read her a story every day when she was a child, typically a classic children's story like an Uncle Wiggily book.

Truman told his biographer Gerald Clarke that Nelle's mother tried to drown her in the bathtub twice as a baby, but her older sisters, Alice and Louise, rescued her. Alice flatly denied that this incident ever happened, as did Nelle. Though she and Truman were best friends in childhood and helped each other as writers after they grew up, they drifted apart in later years. Nelle was very upset by Truman's story, and in a letter to Caldwell Delaney, a friend and former director of the Museum of Mobile, she wrote:

> Truman's vicious lie—that my mother was mentally unbalanced and tried twice to kill me (that gentle soul's reward for having loved him)—was

the first example of his legacy to his friends. Truman left, in the book, something hateful and untrue about every one of them, which more than anything should tell you what was plain to us for more than the last fifteen years of his life—he was paranoid to a terrifying degree. Drugs and alcohol did not cause his insanity, they were the result of it.

Whatever attention Nelle may or may not have gotten from her mother, she received a tremendous amount of love and respect from her father. In his spare time, A. C. loved to play golf, and he wore the same clothes golfing that he wore to the office—fine suit, fedora, dress shoes, and always a pocket watch. Many articles about Harper Lee have stated that Mr. Lee was a direct descendent of General Robert E. Lee, although this is not true. However, he was very much like the character Atticus Finch.

Nelle was two years old when President Herbert Hoover declared, "We in America today are nearer to the final triumph over poverty than ever before in the history of any land. We have not yet reached the goal—but . . . we shall soon, with the help of God, be in sight of the day when poverty will be banished from this nation."

Ironically, President Hoover spoke these words one year before the stock market crash of October 1929, which caused more monetary loss than the total cost of World War I and ignited the Great Depression. Banks closed, businesses failed, and the average family income fell from $2,300 in 1929 to $1,600 by 1935. The Great Depression lasted from 1929 into World War II, spanning most of Nelle's childhood. It was the most severe economic depression "experienced by the industrial Western world." Twenty-three thousand businesses failed in 1929, and that number rose to thirty-two thousand by 1932. In 1931, 2,294 banks with deposits totaling $1.7 billion failed and consequently shut down. By 1933, it was estimated that thirteen million people were unemployed. Shanty-towns called "Hoovervilles" sprang up around the country, along with breadlines and soup kitchens. The phrase "Brother can you spare a dime?" became the national refrain.

Gas was only eighteen cents a gallon, but most folks didn't have extra money for gasoline. One of the main modes of transportation during the Great Depression was called a Hoover cart, named after President Hoover. The cart consisted of a horse pulling two old automobile wheels under a wagon. Nelle's family owned a car, which her father drove in a jerky fashion, pressing the gas, coasting, and then hitting the gas again hard. He thought this method saved on gasoline.

Alice had to leave college in 1929 to come home to work at the newspaper, because there was no more money to pay her tuition. She wound up working at the *Monroe Journal* for seven years. Alice wasn't alone in cutting short her education during the Depression. Many young children were removed from school to find jobs to help their parents earn a living. The next president, Franklin Delano Roosevelt, proclaimed during his March 1933 inauguration address, "Let me assert my firm belief that the only thing we have to fear is fear itself." He introduced a program he called "The New Deal," which focused on "the three R's—relief, recovery, and reform" in order to get the country back on track. Roosevelt and Congress concentrated on everything from unemployment insurance to the National Recovery Act, which helped people get jobs and fair wages. He also created the Works Progress Administration, which generated jobs for people to build highways, public buildings, and parkways, and even to create paintings. Nelle grew up looking at one of the WPA paintings at the Monroeville Post Office—a painting of a farmer and his mules cutting wheat on a hot summer day.

From big cities to small towns, just about everyone suffered during the Great Depression. In Monroeville, Nelle would have seen hobos hopping trains in search of food and work. Nelle once said about the Great Depression that "life was grim for many people who were not only poor but hungry, and their wants were absolutely basic." There wasn't much in the Lee household, but nobody else had much to speak of either.

The Great Depression made a deep and lasting impact on Nelle. Even with all the profits from her book, she made a conscious decision early on to live frugally all her life. Close friends have described her this way:

"She was raised in the Depression in a little Alabama town, and she still has the sensibility." Growing up in Monroeville, there was no public library, no toys, and no extra money for treats.

Truman's absent parents spoiled him with fancy gifts they couldn't afford to win his love, but they left the raising of him to his Alabama relatives. Truman often visited his country cousin, Jennings Carter, known as "Big Boy," who lived outside of Monroeville. When Truman visited Big Boy's family, he saw that they had no running water or electricity, which meant "their lives were ruled by the sun: up at daylight, to bed at dark." Town kids had a little bit more than country kids, since their parents or guardians (as in Truman's case) were employed in law offices and shops, while country people depended on the land for every penny.

Just like the character Walter Cunningham Senior in *To Kill a Mockingbird*, for whom Atticus Finch works out a payment system, farmers or sharecroppers often paid their bills by trading sacks of sweet potatoes or a bushel of tomatoes or a bag of walnuts for services rendered.

* * *

More than anybody else in her family, it was Nelle's big brother, Ed, who used to entertain Nelle and Truman. Nelle said:

> When we were a bit too young to read, Brother, who was a voracious reader, would read many, many stories to us. Then we'd dramatize the stories in our own ways, and Truman would always provide the necessary comic relief to break up the melodrama. Actually, we were the only children on the street of an adult neighborhood. For a while there was the girl across the street, but she didn't live there long. Of course, being the outsiders made it interesting for us. We were able to watch people better. That was our main interest: people watching.

One of Ed's close friends, Charles Ray Skinner, remembered, "Ed was real smart. And he chose his friends, and luckily I was disposed to be one of his friends. He didn't cut up like the rest of us did, but he was a nice guy." He speculated that the reason Ed was more serious in public was because of responsibilities placed on him at home, like watching his little sister. But Ed was a good sport about it. "I'd see them doing sword fights in the front yard, playing, having a good time."

Whether Nelle was sword fighting with Ed or swinging from a tree as Tarzan or making a backyard carnival with Truman and Big Boy, she knew how to create stories and bring them to life. In the last official, unrestricted interview she ever gave about her writing and childhood, Nelle said:

If I went to a film once a month it was pretty good for me, and for all children like me. We had to use our own devices in our play, for our entertainment. We didn't have much money. Nobody had any money. We didn't have toys, nothing was done for us, so the result was we lived in our imagination most of the time. We devised things; we were readers, and we would transfer everything we had seen on the printed page to the backyard in the form of high drama. Did you never play Tarzan when you were a child? Did you never tramp through the jungle or fight the battle of Gettysburg in some form or fashion? We did. Did you never live in a tree house and find the whole world in the branches of a chinaberry tree? We did.

One of the greatest presents Nelle's father ever gave to her and Truman was a black Underwood No. 5 typewriter. Nelle preferred to make up stories and tell them, but Truman convinced her that typing was the way to go, since that was what real writers did. Truman said, "When we were children I had a typewriter and worked every day in a little room I used as an office. I convinced her she ought to write, too, so we would work there each day for two or three hours. She didn't really want to, but I held her to it. We kept up that routine for quite a long time."

One of them would dictate while the other typed. Sometimes, they typed out their stories under the yellow rosebushes in the backyard. Other times, they hauled the twenty-five-pound machine back and forth to each other's houses.

It is not known whether any of Nelle's stories from childhood have survived, but Truman's mother, an alcoholic, burned all of his in a fit of rage after he grew up.

Nelle said that life in a small town provided the most fertile training for storytelling.

> We did not have the pleasure of the theatre, the dance, of motion pictures when they came along. We simply entertained each other by talking. It's quite a thing, if you've never been in or known a small southern town. The people are not particularly sophisticated, naturally. They're not worldly wise in any way. But they tell you a story whenever they see you. We're oral types— we talk.

Truman was Nelle's best friend, no matter how many scraps and scrapes they got into as children. They were even engaged to be married for a short time, but then Truman eloped with another girl. "He must have been about eight," Nelle said. "We were having a fuss. He ran away with another little girl. They hitch-hiked to Evergreen [about twenty miles to the east, past Burnt Corn] but they were back by supper."

Chapter Two

OTHER THAN THE occasional parade or Hog Festival or the rare shopping trip to Evergreen, life in Monroeville operated on a fairly steady routine. Town kids walked home from school at noon for their midday meal, a hot dinner of meat and three—meat and three vegetables. Supper, served at night, was often pancakes or cereal or leftovers from dinner. The paperboy delivered the paper in the afternoon. When children were sick, mothers might make a mustard poultice for a cold, and for the croup, a bad cough, a teaspoon of sugar soaked in moonshine was often the remedy. The grocer at Lazenby's Mercantile on the town square would wring a chicken's neck for a customer and send it home in a paper bag. The town's three switchboard operators connected all the phone calls and even took personal messages. Katz's Department Store was "the store" in town and sold dry goods. The school put on agricultural fairs, and kids dressed up as hams or sacks of fertilizer to march in the parade.

A hot summer day often meant a trip to Hatter's Mill swimming hole with a picnic of hoop cheese, crackers, and RC Cola. When it was especially hot, Truman, Nelle, and Big Boy would get sodas or dopes at the drugstore. A dope was a fountain-made Coca-Cola, with a shot of syrup, ice, and carbonated water. Truman always treated, which meant he charged the bill directly to his aunt Jenny's account so as to save his own coins, which he kept tightly knotted in a handkerchief.

The fiery Alabama sun often shone down on Nelle's head through the green leaves of the chinaberry tree and into the tree house where she read her books. No grown-ups were ever allowed inside—as it should be. Only Truman and Big Boy could enter, and her big brother, Ed, because he read to them, stories full of mystery and adventure like *Tom Swift*, the *Hardy Boys*, and *The Gray Ghost*. Dusty jars of grasshoppers and butterflies sat on a shelf alongside

Truman Capote in the Faulk family garden in Monroeville, Alabama, circa 1927.

old magazines. Other jars held glass marbles "that sparkled with more colors than a dozen rainbows." Nelle read all kinds of books in her tree house. Sometimes, she swapped books with other children, since Monroeville was too small for a town library. Two *Bobbsey Twins* were worth one *Anne of Green Gables*.

"Books were scarce," Nelle wrote in a letter to O magazine in 2006. "There was nothing you could call a public library . . ."

In the house below, her mother spent her days playing the piano and doing daily crossword puzzles in the newspaper. Nelle's mother was a whiz at the *New York Times* crossword, which she could do as quickly as she could move the pencil to fill out each square. During Nelle's childhood, several different black women worked for the Lee family, keeping the house clean and likely functioning as maternal figures to Nelle the way Calpurnia is to Scout in *To Kill a Mockingbird*. They would have been counted on to hold things together when Mrs. Lee was suffering from one of her "nervous disorder" spells. Typically, each woman who worked for the Lee family walked to work from what was then referred to as the Negro section of town. Like all persons of color during that time, she had to enter through the back door. Her salary was approximately a dollar and fifty cents a week, plus meals.

Nelle and Truman loved to do the crosswords together, too. Truman always carried around a pocket dictionary that Nelle's father had given him, along with a little notebook to write down important words or descriptions. He never could just say, "It's hot." He always had to get fancy using words like "barometers."

The children also enjoyed watching jury trials at the Monroe County Courthouse. Sometimes the trials were better than the picture shows, and they were free. Movies at the Monroe Theatre cost a whole dime, plus a nickel for popcorn. By eating a kernel at a time, a kid could make a sack of popcorn last through an entire double-feature. That was called "one-graining it," but times were lean, so Nelle and Truman could afford to go to the picture show only about once a month.

Nelle, Truman, and Big Boy always kept rubber-band guns made of clothespins at the ready. A good shot sailed through the air up to twenty feet or so. Once Truman shot his cousin, whom he called Aunt Jenny and with whom he lived, in the backside, but hid his rubber-band gun so quickly that Nelle and Big

Boy got blamed. Aunt Jenny lit into them, mad as a hornet, before they could explain.

Jenny Faulk was the boss of her family, ordering her brother, two sisters, and Truman around to keep the household on South Alabama Avenue running smoothly. Jenny and her sister, Callie, owned the Faulk Millinery Shop on the town square, which sold all kinds of women's clothing except for shoes, because she didn't want to fool with the smelly feet of customers.

Another cousin of Truman's, Sook, didn't give orders or boss children around like Aunt Jenny, and Nelle, Truman, and Big Boy adored her. When she was young, Sook had suffered a bad fever from which she never fully recovered, making her act childlike. She lived with Truman and Aunt Jenny. Sook never got mad at anybody, and her little dog, Queenie, rarely left her side. She talked about fanciful things, like how the wind blowing through a field of uncut grass was actually "the grass harp" telling stories. When Truman grew up, he wrote several stories inspired by the love he felt for his dreamy cousin, including "A Christmas Memory," "The Thanksgiving Visitor," and a novel, *The Grass Harp*.

* * *

At Monroeville County Elementary School, students knew not to ask too many questions and were expected to meekly digest the material given to them each day. Nelle once explained that country children rarely saw a book before they started school. The town children were "impatient" for the country kids to learn to read, and often "ignored" them because they lagged so far behind.

If students misbehaved, they held out their hands to be smacked with a ruler. At home, Nelle grew up calling her father by his first name, Amasa, the way Scout calls her father "Atticus" in *To Kill a Mockingbird.* One time at school, she got into serious trouble when she addressed a teacher by a first name. When asked to explain her behavior, Nelle pointed out that she had always called her father by his first name. Scandalized, the school immediately ordered her to address every teacher and authority figure with a "Mr." or "Mrs." before the surname. School was not Nelle's favorite place, and Alice once told a reporter that her sister was "extremely bored by the school curriculum" and that teachers regarded her as an "unchallenged student."

Students at Monroeville Elementary School, circa 1945. Nelle was a student in this classroom.

Nelle walked home from school for her dinner in the middle of the day. Country kids could buy a school lunch for a nickel or bring it in a pail. One of Nelle's former classmates, Anne Hines Farish, recalled, "I went home every day for lunch, but the kids who stayed at school ate banana and mayonnaise sandwiches for five cents."

Nelle's principal, James A. York, ran the school from 1919 to 1942. He had a tremendous influence over his students, and in addition to being principal, he was also a preacher, a football coach, and a farmer with Broadway aspirations. He built the school auditorium with the help of some high school boys and put on shows, in which he often played the lead.

A popular and intense schoolyard game at the time was called "Hot Grease in the Kitchen." It began when the first boy arrived at school and declared himself "King of the Kitchen." After that, any boy who walked through the "kitchen" would automatically be wrestled to the ground for trespassing. If the reigning king lost the battle, the winner became the new king.

On one particular morning when Nelle was a first grader, she led the way through her own backyard, which sat adjacent to the playground. Truman, a second grader, followed behind her, and they crossed through "the kitchen"—a sand-bed under a shady oak tree. Older boys were yelling, "Hot Grease in the Kitchen!" Girls were allowed to pass, but no boy was permitted to cross without getting attacked. That morning, Truman, possibly hoping to stir things up, sailed along after Nelle through the "kitchen," only to be tackled and slammed to the ground by the "king," who pinned him and rubbed his face in the sand with the help of some other eager boys. He was a perfect target, dressed in fancy duds from Aunt Jenny's shop.

Nelle pounded her way into the pack to rescue the crying Truman. She was his staunchest defender, but when he irritated her, she didn't have a problem beating "the steam" out of him either. Years later, he said, "She was tough on me," and so were many of his peers who questioned his more delicate ways for a boy.

As far back as Truman could remember, people in Monroeville had thought of him as "a sissy." And Truman often thought it would be easier if he had been born a girl. "I didn't feel as if I were imprisoned in the wrong body . . . I just felt things would be easier for me if I were a girl." But Nelle never let what other people thought influence her decisions about friendship. Truman was her best friend and that was that.

Truman could be tough on his friends too. He had his own set of rules, especially when it came to his personal possessions: "Hands off!" would have been first and foremost. Once, he received a spectacular toy called a Trimotor Ford Airplane, most likely from his absent father, although Truman also claimed he won it in a contest. Whatever the "real story," neither Nelle nor Big Boy could resist the temptation of wanting to ride the fabulous contraption. The plane had a large front wheel and two back wheels and real miniature airplane wings. It was big enough for a child to sit in, a sort of tricycle with airplane wings. But Truman allowed his friends only short rides before he ordered them to get off.

When their stingy friend went away to visit relatives one weekend, Nelle and Big Boy seized their chance. While Sook and Queenie were sleeping, they sneaked the Trimotor Ford out of the bedroom where Truman stored it, and dragged it through the long hallway of the Faulk house to the front porch and down the steps to the road. They pedaled up and down the street, taking turns, but no matter how fast they pedaled they couldn't get it up into the air.

Finally, Big Boy decided that taking off from the slanted roof of the Faulks' barn in the backyard would help make the plane fly. They found Aunt Jenny's tools in the barn and hammered on some three-foot-long lightweight clothes frames to give the plane more wing expansion and balance. Next, they hoisted it up to the roof on a ladder. Nelle was worried that it might not clear the hog pen below, but Big Boy swore he could get it over if she gave him a mighty shove. He put on a helmet and goggles, and decided to aim for a grassy spot near the Joneses' yard next door.

"Pedal, Big Boy! Pedal!" Nelle shouted as she pushed the plane with all her might. But instead of sailing straight out into the wild blue yonder, Big Boy landed smack in the hog pen, spraying mud and filth everywhere and smashing Truman's beautiful airplane.

Terrified that the hogs would eat Big Boy, Nelle held her nose and leapt off the roof of the barn to help him. Covered with manure, they dragged the plane through the pasture and back up to the barn to wash it. They both felt bad about wrecking Truman's toy, not to mention incurring his wrath if he found out the truth. They told him his uncle, a drinker who drove erratically, had run it over, and Truman, devastated at the news, bought the story.

Several years later when Big Boy was twelve years old, he fell off the roof of his own barn and broke his arm. It wasn't set right by a doctor, and forever hung at a ninety-degree angle just like Jem's arm in *To Kill a Mockingbird*. Big Boy didn't let that injury hinder him, though. He grew up to be a pilot and flew planes in World War II, and then became a crop duster in Alabama for decades. He was even inducted into the Alabama Aeronautics Hall of Fame. Truman flew all over the world as an adult, but throughout her life, Nelle has steadfastly chosen trains over airplanes.

In 1932, Nelle's everyday life was forever changed when Truman's mother decided she wanted her only son to leave Monroeville and move to New York City to join her and her new husband, Joe Capote. Before Truman moved, he decided to throw a Halloween party as a going-away celebration. He wanted the event to be

"One that will be so much fun and so exciting that people in Monroeville will remember me and the party forever."

He intended to invite everybody, including one black friend, John White, which was unheard of in Monroeville in 1932. Blacks and whites did not attend parties together, unless blacks were working at a party hosted by whites. Truman wanted John to dress up in a white suit and be in charge of the apple bobbing contest.

Truman also invited the most mysterious young man in the neighborhood, Alfred "Son" Boulware, who rarely left his house. Typically, all people saw of Son was a pale white hand reaching out from behind a screen door to retrieve the afternoon newspaper. More than a few folks in Monroeville say that Son Boulware may have been the inspiration for Boo Radley in *To Kill a Mockingbird*, but others say most towns had their own versions of Boo Radley.

Son hadn't always been a recluse. When Nelle was two years old, in 1928, Son was in high school, and one night he and some boys destroyed school property. They were caught, and, much like Boo Radley's father in *To Kill a Mockingbird*, Son Boulware's father convinced the judge to release his son from police custody and promised to discipline the boy himself. The judge agreed, and Mr. Boulware took his son home and never let him attend school again. Gradually Son stopped going out at all.

Throughout Nelle's childhood, the Boulware place stood unpainted and dreary on South Alabama Avenue, full of shadowy secrets to spark the imaginations of children like Nelle and Truman. Ed Lee's good friend Charles Ray Skinner called Son Boulware's life "a tragedy." Skinner's older brother knew Son and described him as one of the smartest boys in school. His classmates used to drop by and slide their math homework under the door for his help. But eventually those boys went off to college, and Son stayed home. His sisters denied that he was a recluse and said that he liked going for Sunday drives with the family, but the majority of people in Monroeville who remember him said he rarely, if ever, ventured outside.

But in the fall of 1932, Son and his sister, Sally, accepted Truman's invitation, and Son decided to dress as a robot. Costumed as what can best be described as a hobo, Nelle smudged her face with chimney soot and red lipstick and wore a man's shirt. Big Boy did the same. Truman painted his face yellow and dressed like Fu Manchu, because he'd read about the Chinese Tong wars in California, which involved Chinese mafia gangs fighting over opium dens, gambling parlors, and other illegal activities.

The party was going well. Aunt Jenny had a phonograph—a new machine at the time—and one record to play, and folks thought it was marvelous. But the local chapter of the Klu Klux Klan (KKK) had heard that John White had been invited as a guest to the party, and decided to pay Aunt Jenny's house a visit. The KKK was especially forceful in the South, where the group originated after the Civil War. They tried to enforce their views by using violence and intimidation methods ranging from cross burning to tarring and feathering to lynching. They saw themselves as "one-hundred percent American" and anyone who disagreed with them was un-American. The KKK was not only anti-black, they were also anti-Catholic, anti-Semitic, anti-Asian—basically anti-anybody who didn't agree with their white supremacist values.

When the KKK showed up that night on South Alabama Avenue, they surrounded a man dressed as a robot in the Lee yard. They suspected he was a black man, but in fact, it was Son Boulware. His sister Sally raced to get help at the Faulk house. Meanwhile, Mr. Lee, who was home at the time, came outside to find Son sobbing in the front yard, his mask off. "I wasn't going to hurt anybody. I was coming to the party as a robot, that's all," Son explained.

Mr. Lee confronted the leader of the KKK and said, "See what your foolishness has done? You've scared this boy half to death because you wanted to believe something that wasn't true. You ought to be ashamed of yourselves."

Years later, Truman remembered Son only as a terribly shy young man in the neighborhood who left presents for children in the knothole in a tree. He said both he and Nelle put him in their stories. Truman said, "In my original version of *Other Rooms, Other Voices*, I had that same man living in the house that used to leave things in trees, and then I took that out. He was a real man, and he lived just down the road from us. We used to go and get those things out of the trees. Everything she wrote about it is absolutely true."

Son never moved out of his house, and he died of tuberculosis at the age of forty-two in 1952. He is buried at the Baptist Cemetery in Monroeville, where his grave marker states: "TO LIVE IN THE HEARTS WE LEAVE BEHIND IS NOT TO DIE."

After the party, Truman moved to New York City, and Nelle no longer had a best friend next door. But he spent summers with the Faulks, so he wasn't gone entirely, much as Dill came home to Scout and Jem each summer in *To Kill a Mockingbird*.

Chapter Three

THE COLOR OF a person's skin meant everything in Monroeville, as it did throughout the South, where Jim Crow Laws were fully enforced. A black person was not allowed to marry a white person. Blacks and whites did not worship together. At a white funeral, black people sat up in the church balcony, just as they did at the County Courthouse and at the Monroe Theatre. It was illegal for blacks and whites to eat in the same room at a restaurant or to shoot a game of pool together. Separate schools, separate cells in prison, separate railroad cars, separate mental hospitals, separate entrances when the circus came to town. Blacks were not allowed in public libraries and could not check out books. If a black woman wanted to buy a new dress, a white shopkeeper typically insisted that she try it on over her own clothes.

One of the most brutal examples of the racial injustice of that era came in the case of the Scottsboro Boys, which was covered in national newspapers from 1931 to 1949, in which nine black men were accused of raping two white women. The nine black men, traveling to find work, had been on a freight train bound for Alabama when a fight broke out with a group of white men, while the train was in Tennessee. By the time the train arrived in Paint Rock, Alabama, word of the fight had spread, and a mob had gathered. Two white women, also on the train, accused the black men of rape, and Governor Benjamin Meek Miller had to call in the National Guard to maintain control and protect the men.

In a series of grossly biased, unfair trials that finished in record time, all nine men, including the youngest, age thirteen, were sentenced to death by Alabama's infamous electric chair, "Yellow Mama." Doctors had testified under oath that no rapes took place, but the juries convicted the men anyway. The rapid rate of the trials and death sentences sparked national attention and outrage.

The Communist Party's International Labor Defense (ILD) stepped in to appeal the decisions and clear

Two of the five Scottsboro Boys, Olen Montgomery (in glasses) and Eugene Williams, arriving at New York's Penn Station, 1937.

the men of all false charges. As it became apparent that the Scottsboro Boys had been framed, the National Association for the Advancement of Colored People (NAACP) also tried to become involved in helping the men. The NAACP had been reluctant to defend them initially, partly because it didn't want to be associated with a radical group like the Communist Party. But each organization wanted to be seen as the rescuer of the Scottsboro Boys by the public. Ultimately, the NAACP, the ILD, and other organizations formed a delicate alliance, the Scottsboro Defense Committee, to help the Scottsboro Boys win their freedom.

Dr. Claudia Durst Johnson explained the atmosphere in the United States around the time of the Scottsboro Boys case.

> The economic collapse of the 1930s resulted in ferocious rivalry for the very few jobs that became available. Consequently, the ill will between black and white people (which had existed ever since the Civil War) intensified, as each group competed with the other for the few available jobs. One result was that incidents of lynchings—primarily of African Americans—continued. Here, lynching should be defined as the murder of a person by a group of people who set themselves up as judge, jury, and executioner outside the legal system.

If Governor Miller had not called in the National Guard, it is very likely that all nine men would have been lynched, given the racial climate of northern Alabama and the rest of the South.

Although the alleged rapes occurred in 1931, the

Scottsboro Boys trials stretched out until 1949 with appeals, retrials, and pardons. The defendants' attorney for the appeal, Samuel Leibowitz, known in parts of the South as "a Jew lawyer from New York City," did not win any of the trials, but he ultimately saved the lives of the accused and turned the eye of the world on Alabama, according to Alabama historian, Dr. Wayne Flynt. Eventually all the men went free, but it came with a terribly high price—their lives. They spent precious years waiting through trials, retrials, appeals, and pardons before it was all over. "There are heroes in this story," Flynt said. "But that's the footnote to this story. The tragedy of this are nine boys' lives hopelessly, eternally interrupted, sent cascading down roads of terror and imprisonment. I don't think there's any way to see this story but as a great tragedy."

In the fall of 1933, two and a half years after the Scottsboro Boys were arrested, a similar trial was making news in Monroeville. The accused was Walter Lett, a black man. His alleged crime was raping a white woman.

Nelle was seven years old when the Lett trial was

going on, and she would likely have heard it discussed in her home. She had also been an avid reader of the newspaper from a very early age. Walter Lett stated that he was innocent and did not know the woman who had accused him. A. C. Lee published the following story about Lett in the *Monroe Journal* on November 9, 1933.

NEGRO HELD FOR
ATTACKING WOMAN

Walter Lett, alias Walter Brown, negro, is being held for assault on Mrs. Naomi Lowery, a white woman. The attack is alleged to have occurred on Thursday afternoon near the brick factory south of Monroeville. The attack was not reported until Friday and an investigation followed immediately by the sheriff's office. The negro was captured on Saturday and taken into custody. Fearing that an attempt would be made to lynch the negro by a mob following the news of the attack, Sheriff Sawyer took the negro to jail in Greenville for safekeeping.

* * *

Several months later on March 29, 1934, Lett was found guilty and condemned to death, with a verdict rendered at 9 P.M. in the courtroom. But the execution did not take place. Shortly after Lett was convicted and sentenced to death, many of the leading white townspeople in Monroeville had begun writing letters in his defense, because they did not believe that he had committed this crime. Alabama governor Miller twice ordered Lett's electrocution to be delayed, basing his decision on the letters and statements from the upstanding citizens of Monroeville. Finally he commuted the death sentence to life in prison. It is not clear why he didn't dismiss the charges altogether, although it was probably too dangerous for him to do so. During this time, it was an understood fact that any white "leading citizen" who defended a black man could expect a visit from the KKK.

Today, the Monroe County Courthouse keeps all files and transcripts of trials in chronological order in a fil-

The old Monroe County Courthouse, Monroeville, Alabama, 1998.

ing room. Around 1998, some scholars decided to read the transcripts of the Lett trial to compare it with the fictionalized Tom Robinson trial in *To Kill a Mockingbird*. So they went to the courthouse to search through the old files. They found transcripts and files for every trial that took place during the twentieth century, except for those destroyed when the courthouse burned down in 1928. They located all of the trial transcripts and files from the year 1934. All, that is, but one. The Lett folder was missing, and still is. In the late 1990s, Harper Lee told a biographer of Richard Wright that the Walter Lett trial was the inspiration for Tom Robinson.

As for Walter Lett, he was transferred from state prison to a hospital after he contracted tuberculosis. He died in state custody in 1937.

The Walter Lett trial took place over approximately nine months of Nelle's childhood, and the Scottsboro Boys trials dominated the news well into her adulthood. Without question, these trials influenced the fictionalized trial of Tom Robinson. But there was a third case, a trial that occurred before Nelle was born, that may have informed *To Kill a Mockingbird* because of its personal connection to her father. In his first and only criminal case, Mr. Lee was appointed to defend two black men accused of murdering a white storekeeper. He was a new lawyer and lost the case. Both men were hanged. The story of the 1919 trial read as follows on Christmas Day, 1919, in the *Monroe Journal*.

✳ ✳ ✳

TWO NEGROES EXECUTED

For the second time within a period of forty years, Monroe County has had a legal execution for the commission of crime, Frank Ezell and Brown Ezell, father and son, on Friday, December 19, expiated on the gallows under the sentence of the court the murder of Mr. William H. Northrup.

Morbid curiosity drew a large crowd to town on the fateful day, but few were admitted within the prison walls, while those outside could catch but an occasional word that fell from the lips of the accused men and realize only in imagination the gruesome task that fell to the lot of Sheriff Russell and his assistants.

Both negroes made statements on the gallows, the older man protesting his innocence of any complicity in the crime. The younger made full confession, asserting that he alone was responsible and that his punishment was just. The Journal spares its readers the frightful details of the execution. Let us hope that there may never again be occasion for a similar sentence of law.

It's possible that all of the trials together inspired Nelle to create her own fictionalized version. Or maybe the Tom Robinson trial was a way of honoring her father. A minister in town approached Alice Lee decades ago, asking about "the year of Tom Robinson's trial. He said he wanted to go down to the newspaper office and read about it. And I had to say there was no trial. He really was upset. How could anyone write so convincingly about something that never happened? Well, I told him, my sister's an author and we're not."

Chapter Four

NELLE DIDN'T APPEAR to be interested in flirting with boys or dating, like a majority of teenage girls. Instead of climbing up inside the clock tower to spy on boys, she preferred viewing them on the ground in games of football. One afternoon, Nelle convinced some boys to let her play in their scrimmage. One of the local football heroes did not want her to play and said so, but she ignored him—at first. When Nelle's friend A. B. Blass passed her the ball, she took off toward the goal line and stiff-armed the football hero, knocking him under a tree. When he protested that they were only playing touch football, Nelle replied, "I thought we were going to play ball!"

Nelle still saw Truman during his summer visits to Monroeville. One time he arrived in a chauffer-driven Buick, according to A. B. Blass, who was playing baseball with his friends in the empty lot next to the Courthouse.

"Can I play ball with you fellows?" Truman asked when he got out of the car. But nobody wanted Truman on their team since he swung a bat like he was chopping wood, and he never paid attention when playing out in right field. Balls would sail right past him, and he'd never even notice.

Finally, Bass said that Truman sighed, "Sure is hot. Would y'all like a set-up? My treat." This was a ten-cent drink at the soda fountain, and all the boys decided to take him up on his offer.

Once at the soda fountain, Blass said, "We either ordered double Limeade or Dope. After we finished our set-ups, we picked Truman to play on our team." But whenever he was in town after that and wanted to play ball, Bass said the boys always demanded a set-up first. Naturally Truman charged everything to Aunt Jenny's account.

Nelle's most influential high school teacher, Miss Gladys Watson, became her friend and mentor for life. Miss Watson lived across the street from the Lee family, and she was the one who introduced Nelle to British literature. Miss Watson (who married much later in life to become Mrs. Gladys Watson Burkett) emphasized the three Cs in her teaching: "clarity, coherence, and cadence." She expected students to study the rules of grammar, and if they didn't get it right the first time, they rewrote their papers until every comma splice or run-on sentence was eradicated. Nelle adored her teacher and loved nineteenth-century British authors, especially Jane Austen, who became a tremendous influence on her. Nelle later told an interviewer that she wanted to be the Jane Austen of south Alabama.

Monroe County High School had no monthly newspaper nor even a yearbook where a student's creative writing might have been noticed, so it is not known if Miss Watson thought Nelle was going to be a writer when she was a student. However, it is clear that she instilled a love of language and reading in her pupil. Nelle said years later, "There's no substitute for the love of language, for the beauty of an English sentence. There's no substitute for struggling, if a struggle is needed, to make an English sentence as beautiful as it should be."

Nelle spent many hours in the school library, reading those beautiful sentences. The town had built a brand-new high school in 1936, and Nelle was a student there from 1940 to 1944.

On January 25, 1940, a raging fire in the middle of the night burned down Truman's family's house next door to the Lees'. It was one of the coldest nights of the year in Monroeville, with the temperature dipping down to eleven degrees. Fire and smoke filled the neighborhood, and by the time the Volunteer Fire Department had extinguished the fire, the house had burned to the ground. Neighbors soon appeared with blankets and food to help the Faulks, as was the custom when anybody in town was in trouble. The family escaped unharmed except for Queenie, Sook's dog, who died in the fire. The home that Nelle, Truman, and Big Boy had spent so many hours in as children was gone.

On December 7, 1941, when Nelle was a sophomore in high school, the Japanese bombed Pearl Harbor. The very next day, the United States declared war on Japan

A close-up of Nelle's tenth-grade class at Monroe County High School, 1941. She is standing on the far right.

and entered into World War II. During the following four years, over sixteen million Americans served in the armed forces, including Nelle's brother, Ed, who joined the Army Air Corps at age twenty-one. Many other boys with whom Nelle grew up fought, too: A. B. Blass, George Thomas Jones, Charles Ray Skinner, and Big Boy. Nelle was thirteen when the war began, and it ended during her freshman year at Huntingdon College, in 1945.

During those wartime years, Nelle's family, like most families in the United States, had to ration butter, sugar, meat, gasoline, and many other products in order to support the war effort. Scrap metal, from bottle tops to car bumpers, was donated to help, too. Mr. Lee and his law office sold war bonds, which were similar to today's savings bonds. Alice volunteered for the Red Cross. Louise was married and living with her new baby in Eufaula, Alabama, while her husband was stationed overseas. Mobile, Alabama, just a hundred miles south of Monroeville, became a boomtown, with ammunition factories springing up everywhere. Women also entered the workforce like never before, since the men were away at war.

Nelle graduated from high school in 1944 and followed Alice's lead by attending Huntingdon College in Montgomery, Alabama. Alice was a sister to look up to and learn from, which Nelle made a gallant effort to do especially as an undergraduate, when she thought she would become a lawyer like her father and sister.

In 1937 Alice had moved to Birmingham, Alabama, to take a job with the Internal Revenue Service in its Social Security division. She resumed her education at that time, which had been interrupted by the Great Depression, by attending night school at the Birmingham School of Law. She passed the Bar exam in 1943 and left her IRS job because a new position had opened for her back in Monroeville—in her father's law firm.

Today, at age ninety-seven, Alice still practices law in that same firm, Barnett, Bugg, & Lee.

Nelle's freshman year was her first time away from home, and while she hadn't acted like the majority of girls in Monroeville, she fit in even less with the young ladies at Huntingdon. Smoking cigarettes was quite common among the coeds at Huntingdon, but not the pipe that Nelle was seen smoking in her dorm room. She preferred brushing her hair to curling it, she didn't wear makeup, and she wore Bermuda shorts instead of skirts whenever possible. Girls were expected to dress in evening gowns at least once a month for dinners, and Nelle avoided these events. One of her classmates, Catherine Helms, described her this way: "She wasn't worried about how her hair looked or whether she had a date on Friday night like the rest of us were. I don't remember her sitting around and giggling and being silly and talking about what our weddings were going to be like—that's what teenage girls talked about. She was not part of our 'girl group.' She never had what we call in the South 'finishing touches.'"

Nelle, however, excelled in her classes and academic work, making the dean's list her first semester. But what is most remembered about her is her great athleticism. She could spike a volleyball and was one of the top soccer players at the school. Nelle was simply ahead of her time in that she chose to be comfortable with who she was rather than try to fit in. She refused to march to the same drumbeat of marriage and children that the majority of women were expected to heed in that era. Her early stories reveal a writer ready to tackle subjects that had nothing to do with love or romance or the latest styles.

Her closest friend at Huntingdon was a young woman named Jeanne Foote, and in Jeanne she found a friend with whom to discuss literature and politics, subjects that didn't seem to appeal much to other students at Huntingdon. In an interview with Charles Shields, Foote said, "Those conversations were very important to me. I don't think that there were others at Huntingdon—whom I knew and had ready access to—who had these same interests."

Nelle wrote some of her first articles for the campus newspaper, *The Huntress*, and published some of her first pieces of fiction in the college literary magazine, *The Prelude*. Two of her fictional stories, "A Wink at Justice" and "Nightmare," feature courtroom settings and lynchings.

"A Wink at Justice" opens in a courtroom thick with "tobacco smoke, cheap hair oil, and perspiration." The jury is a group of "august boys" with cuspidors at strategic spitting distance. Eight black men are on trial for gambling behind a warehouse. After a quick study of eight pairs of hands, Judge Hanks dismisses three of the men and charges the other five with sixty days in jail. The judge notes that the three men had corns on their hands, which meant they were hardworking, family men. He explains, "It was the ones with soft, smooth hands that I was after. They're the ones who gamble professionally, and we don't need that sort of thing around here. . . ."

In "Nightmare," a child recalls witnessing a lynching, and feeling icy cold in the burning August heat. After the hanging, passersby discuss it like a sporting event. " . . . Best hanging I've seen in twenty years. . . ."

It is clear from these two short pieces that Nelle was already beginning to experiment with the setting and action that would become the very heart of *To Kill a Mockingbird.*

Chapter Five

AFTER HER FRESHMAN year at Huntingdon, Nelle transferred to the University of Alabama in Tuscaloosa to study law, since Huntingdon did not offer a law degree. With her father and Alice both lawyers, Nelle decided law would be the best route for her. By 1945, veterans from the war began returning to college, and having classes with older men created a more serious atmosphere on campus. Nelle also decided to pledge Chi Omega, a sorority "that specialized in blondes" according to the yearbook. Nelle kept her thick, dark hair short and dressed in plain, tailored clothes. The student body was mostly "Greek," meaning that college girls pledged sororities and college boys pledged fraternities. Perhaps that was why Nelle decided to pledge—to make friends and fit in more than she had at Huntingdon.

Nelle, second from the right, at the University of Alabama in Tuscaloosa, circa 1946.

Nelle, the tomboy of the sorority, wrote about an incident when the girls thought they heard a burglar in the middle of the night at the Chi O house. They elected Nelle to explain the danger to the police and the night watchman.

"Finally someone hit upon the bright idea of calling the police. The police and the night watchman came an hour later. After screaming at them the pertinent data (the police) reached the admired conclusion that they ought to search the house. I was chosen to escort them through the premises, and when we got up to the attic the night watchman gave me his flashlight and said, 'You go first.'"

After a year with the Chi Omega sisters, Nelle moved out of the sorority house and into the women's dormitory. She just couldn't fit in with the sorority girls, but she did find a place to belong when she joined the campus newspaper, *The Crimson White*. There, she discovered a "second home" and a group of more like-minded students, including those who hated bigotry and the Klan with a passion. After pitching ideas to the editor of the campus newspaper and hanging around in the summer while other students went home, she began to publish a column in *The Crimson White* the summer of 1946 called "Caustic Comment." She followed that up by becoming the editor of the college humor magazine called *The Rammer Jammer* from the fall of 1946 until the spring of 1947. This is what was said in *The Crimson White* about her tenure as editor of the magazine.

In case you've seen an intellectual looking young lady cruising down University avenue toward Pug's dressed in tan, laden with law books, sleepy and in a hurry and wondered who she is—she's Nelle Harper Lee.

Miss Lee is editor of the Rammer Jammer (if you've never heard of the Rammer Jammer, it's not Miss Lee's fault), a law student, a Chi Omega, a writer, a Triangle member, a chain smoker, and a witty conversationalist.

She is a traditional and impressive figure as she strides down the corridor of New Hall at all hours attired in men's green striped pajamas. Quite frequently she passes out candy to unsuspecting freshmen; when she emerges from their rooms they have subscribed to the Rammer Jammer.

Her Utopia is a land with the culture of England and the government of Russia; her idea of heaven is a place where diligent law students and writers ascend after death and can stay up forever without Benzedrine.

Wild about football, she played center on the fourth grade team in Monroeville, her hometown. Her favorite person is her sister "Bear."

Lawyer Lee will spend her future in Monroeville. As for literary aspirations she says, "I shall probably write a book some day. They all do."

Clearly, Nelle was already preparing for her life as a writer and editor, even as a full-time law student. Her self-deprecating sense of humor is evident, and it's not surprising that students looked forward to each new issue of the *Rammer Jammer*.

One of the most respected professors on the University of Alabama campus was Shakespearian scholar Hudson Strode, with whom Nelle studied. She loved Shakespeare and later said, "I don't know what kind of teacher he was, but I know one thing; if you met even half of his demands, you received something in return that stays with you the rest of your life." Strode also taught a creative writing workshop that students had to submit work to in order to be considered. Spaces were limited, and the selection process was very competitive. It is not known if Nelle ever applied to Strode's workshop, but "he claimed her after the publication of 'Mockingbird.'"

The combination of Gladys Watson Burkett and Hudson Strode naturally would have contributed to Nelle's decision to become an exchange student in England, which became a very formative experience in her life. She was accepted into a summer program at Oxford and set sail on the *Marine Jumper* in the summer of 1948. On the journey across the Atlantic Ocean, Nelle and the other students spent their days listening to talks about the course of study at Oxford and watching films to help them get ready for the study abroad program. When she arrived in Plymouth Harbor on June 25, she was immediately struck by the multitude of British accents so foreign to her Southern ear. She also had to get used to a whole new money system that used pounds instead of dollars, but she was on a grand adventure. She and the other students took a four-hour train ride to Oxford University, and soon she was attending lectures on Virginia Woolf, T. S. Eliot, Thomas Mann, Gerard Manley Hopkins, Jane Austen, and Jean-Paul Sartre. Oxford, with its intimate tutorials and view of Christ Church, built in the 1500s, was a whole new world for Nelle. Her sister Alice said she fell in love with England.

The *Monroe Journal*, which reported on the travels of all its citizens, whether they were headed to Dothan, Alabama, or Oxford, England, announced her trip on April 29, 1948:

MISS NELLE LEE CHOSEN
TO ATTEND OXFORD

Miss Nelle Lee, University of Alabama law student and daughter of Mr. and Mrs. A. C. Lee of Monroeville, has been accepted as an exchange student at Oxford University in England during the coming summer. She will sail from New York on June 16th. Miss Lee, a junior in the school of Law at Alabama, is the only student from Alabama to be selected to attend Oxford under the exchange setup whereby English students will attend American colleges during the summer. Her selection was made by the International Education Exchange in New York.

Nelle spent that summer of 1948 exploring the cobblestone streets and treading the same paths of writers she loved and admired. She could soak up British literature and discuss it with other scholars who understood her passion for language and stories. After her tenure in England, she began her last year at the University of Alabama, but on the verge of graduation with a law degree, Nelle knew in her heart she did not want to be a lawyer. She was soon faced with one of the most difficult decisions of her life.

Truman's first book, *Other Rooms, Other Voices,* had been published in 1948. After her summer in England, Nelle was back again in her dorm room at the University of Alabama in Tuscaloosa. The *Chicago Tribune* had just reviewed Truman's novel, calling it, "A short novel which is as dazzling a phenomenon as has burst on the literary scene in the last ten years."

Truman had done what he had set out to do—become a writer. And it was exactly what Nelle wanted to do, too, even if her family thought a law degree was the wiser choice for her. But England had made such a tremendous impression upon her that a career in law could not compete with her love of literature and writing.

Outside her window at college, groups of girls in camel-hair coats might have strolled by, their laughter like little bells in the air. The coeds' high heels surely clicked along the sidewalk on their way to a sorority or fraternity party. The Crimson Tide backdrop of Alabama football and the sultry humidity of Tuscaloosa couldn't have contrasted more greatly to the spires of Christ Church Cathedral at Oxford swirling up into the mist. Nelle had loved everything about England. Still, everybody knew that the place for writers was New York City, the heart of the publishing world.

But whenever she brought up the subject of moving to New York to her family, she faced a wall of resistance. If she had to write, her father insisted she'd be much happier in Monroeville, writing for the *Monroe Journal*. Writing novels in New York wasn't considered a practical profession, and she'd do much better to become a lawyer. Besides, Mr. Lee thought a small-town girl like Nelle would get lost in a big place like New York. Alice also thought she should stay in Alabama and be more of a help to the family—a role Alice had assumed much of her life.

Still, no matter how scary the thought of New York

was, the notion of staying in Alabama for the rest of her life scared Nelle even more. She knew she wouldn't be happy hanging up a sign on the law office building that said A. C. LEE AND DAUGHTERS. She wouldn't be happy being anything but a writer. She'd had her first real taste of the world in Oxford, reading everything she could get her hands on. Nelle envisioned a bigger life for herself than the one in Monroeville. She also knew if she graduated, she would feel compelled to join the family law firm. On the other hand, her family had made sacrifices for her, helping her through college and the summer in England, paying for her tuition. Her mother's health wasn't strong, and both Alice and her father made it clear how much they needed her. Louise was married, and so was Ed.

But Nelle decided she would prove to them she could do it on her own. She would not ask for financial support (nor would it be offered). She would get a regular job and find a cheap apartment. She wouldn't be the first poor writer in New York City.

Nelle was twenty-three years old, and it took great courage to go against her family's wishes and quit law school, but as Alice said years later, she had "the itch" to write. She was leaving everything that was familiar to live alone in a city where she knew virtually no one. But the truth was she did know one person in New York City.

His name was Truman.

Chapter Six

RIGHT AFTER DROPPING out of the University of Alabama, Nelle returned home to Monroeville to work and save money before moving to New York City. Truman had encouraged her to leave Alabama and head north. It is not known if he thought that she should move immediately, but it's likely that he understood her need to work and save money. He was in a position to introduce her to the New York literary scene. It is also likely that he wrote her many letters, as he was a prolific letter writer, but none between the two friends have survived or been made public.

Nobody in Monroeville succeeded in talking Nelle out of moving to New York, and she boarded a train in Birmingham bound for New York in 1949. Alice and Mr. Lee accompanied her to the station to see her off. An article ran in the *Monroe Journal* about her departure:

MISS LEE ACCEPTS POSITION
IN NEW YORK

Miss Nelle Harper Lee, former Monroeville resident, has recently accepted a position as assistant editor of the School Executive and the annual publication of the American School and University Publishing Company in New York City. Miss Lee attended the University of Alabama before going to New York.

Nelle made her new home at 1539 York Avenue, two blocks from the East River. It was a cold-water flat with a fire escape outside her window. She cooked her supper on a hot plate—a single burner—and ate mostly soup and stew. There was no running hot water, and renters kept warm by using either electric space heaters or kerosene heaters. The fire escape was a lovely refuge where Nelle could read books or sit outside on summer evenings.

Nelle and Truman occasionally got together with a group of Alabama transplants living in New York. They would bring a bottle of bourbon and join the party, although it doesn't appear that Nelle was close with many in the group other than Truman. Eugene Walter, an Alabama novelist, described the gatherings: "All the Southerners in New York would get together about every ten days or two weeks and cry over Smithfield ham. There was a community, like a religious group except it wasn't a church. Southerners always, by secret gravity, find themselves together. . . . You always knew, if there was any kind of trouble, that was like [having] cousins in town." It must have been a comfort to Nelle, after a long workweek, to listen to the rhythm and cadence of voices from her home state with her best friend from childhood.

Another fellow Southern transplant and writer, Joseph Mitchell, observed: "Until I came to New York City I had never lived in a town with a population of more than 2,699, and I was alternately delighted and frightened out of my wits."

Nelle quite likely shared Mitchell's sentiments and could have said the same about the population

A typical New York City street scene, circa 1950.

of Monroeville. She learned to navigate Manhattan and explored her neighborhood of German-Czech-Romanian neighbors, which was filled with pubs, coffee shops, delis, and even German movie theaters. She could wander from neighborhood to neighborhood, soaking up the sounds and smells and languages of each block.

If everybody knew everybody's business in Monroeville, New York was the perfect place for Nelle to be invisible. She came and went as she pleased, without remark. Sometimes when a writer leaves the familiarity of home, both distance and time make memories come sharply into focus. This was the case for Nelle. She began to reach back into her childhood to craft her stories.

When she wasn't writing or working, the Metropolitan Museum of Art was one of her favorite places to go. She also loved going to movies, and New York always had plenty. Nelle's sense of humor is illustrated by the scene when she and friend Ruth Waller attended a movie revival in New York of an old film, *The Fall of the House of Usher.* The acting was so contrived and the lines so heavy-handed that Nelle couldn't help adding her own absurd dialogue along with the movie. She and Waller were harshly reprimanded by the movie management, but were laughing too hard to take much notice. Waller later wrote: "Nelle Lee is no ordinary person. She is an iconoclast. She had an innate hatred of 'phoniness' and she made no bones about those she liked (who were few) and those she loathed (who were legion). She was one of the most honest and straight-forward persons I ever knew, in a city not noted for those virtues."

Although the *Monroe Journal* stated that Nelle had accepted an editorial job for a publishing company, she also worked at a bookstore. But it didn't provide the literary life she was seeking, nor did she earn enough money to live on in New York City. She found a better job working for Eastern Airlines by 1950. Once she was trained, she switched to British Overseas Air Corporation (BOAC) to work as a reservations clerk. Nelle got an employee discount on tickets, which meant there was the potential for trips back to England, but she never seemed to have extra money to travel except back home.

Her mother's health was in gradual decline, and Nelle needed to go home often. Working for BOAC Airlines was the perfect kind of job, because at the end of the day, she could leave her work at the office and focus on writing at home.

Nelle had hopes like any other writer, and she also had discipline and worked each night after work. She also wrote letters home; her correspondence with friends and family may have been a way of warming up to real writing. Strong coffee helped, too. She always wrote first drafts in longhand.

Nelle couldn't afford a fancy desk in her tiny apartment, so she used a door laid across two sawhorses as a writing table. She lived frugally, saving every penny for rent, groceries, cigarettes, pencils, paper, and typewriter ribbons so she wouldn't have to ask her family for money. She wanted to prove she could live in New York on her own terms, without any help from anybody. She and Truman met occasionally in places like Central Park, but he was very busy with his new novel, *The Grass Harp*, which he also adapted into a play that opened in 1952. Still, he encouraged her writing and introduced her to people in the arts and literature community. But she never showed anybody her stories in those early years and often destroyed rough drafts that weren't up to her standards.

Nelle's mother died in a hospital in Selma on June 2, 1951. Nelle was twenty-five years old. She went home, but before the family even had time to finish grieving, they suffered a much harder loss. Six weeks after the death of Frances Lee, Nelle's beloved brother, Ed, died of a brain aneurysm on July 12, 1951. He had been recalled to active duty in the Army Air Force and was at Maxwell Airfield. A little out of shape, he had played a very intense game of softball the day before, and doctors thought this might have been a contributing factor. Ed left behind his wife and two small children. The loss of their mother was painful, but Ed's death devastated Nelle's entire family. She may have briefly considered moving back to Monroeville, but home for her had become New York. After these terrible losses, she began writing fragments of what would later become *To Kill a Mockingbird*, and the loving way she created the character of Jem was perhaps a way of keeping a little part of her own brother with her.

After almost eight years in New York, working at and practicing her craft, Nelle was finally ready to submit her short stories to a literary agent. Her close friends Joy and Michael Brown, whom she met through Truman, had recommended Annie Laurie Williams, but Williams was actually a film agent. However, Williams's husband, Maurice Crain, was a literary agent, who worked in the office next door to his wife's. Nelle arrived with her collection of stories, but she was too scared to go inside the building. "I walked around the block three times before I could muster the courage to go in and give the stories to the agent. At the time, I was very shy. Finally, I rushed in, left the manuscripts with the secretary, and left. I prayed for a quick death, and forgot about it."

Maurice Crain liked her short stories but thought he'd be able to place only one, called "Snow-on-the-Mountain," about a boy tearing up a cranky old lady's flowers. He then discussed the idea of Nelle's writing a novel. She said she would think about it. The idea had occurred to her during her seven years in New York, but she was working full-time and writing short stories, so her time was precious. Then a kind of Christmas miracle happened.

After meeting with Crain, Nelle began working on a novel that she called *Go Set a Watchman*. Earning a living and struggling to write a book dominated Nelle's life, but in December 1957, she received a tremendously generous gift from Michael and Joy Brown. Michael was a lyricist who had collaborated with Truman on his story "House of Flowers," which became a musical on Broadway. Nelle had become very close to the Browns and their children, and since she couldn't go home for Christmas that year because she had to work at the airline on Christmas Day, she spent Christmas Eve and morning with them.

In an essay published in *McCall's* magazine about that holiday, called "Christmas to Me," Nelle wrote:

I missed Christmas away from home, I thought. What I really missed was a memory, an old memory of people long since gone, of my grandparents' house bursting with cousins, smilax, and holly. I missed the sound of hunting boots, the sudden open-door gusts of chilly air that cut through the aroma of pine needles and oyster dressing. I missed my brother's night-before-Christmas mask of rectitude and my father's bumblebee bass humming "Joy to the World."

While everyone was opening presents, it became

clear that there was nothing under the tree for Nelle, and she was trying very hard not to feel disappointed. But finally Joy said, "We haven't forgotten you. Look on the tree."

On the tree was an envelope addressed to Nelle, and inside was a note: "You have one year off from your job to write whatever you please. Merry Christmas." There was also a blank check inside. Nelle was to fill in whatever amount she needed to live for a year, so she would be able to write without having to worry about a full-time job. Nelle was shocked to her core by the gift and said, "It's a fantastic gamble. It's such a great risk."

Michael looked at her and said, "No, honey. It's not a risk. It's a sure thing."

Nelle wrote to a friend in Alabama about her present from the Browns:

The one stern string attached is that I will be subjected to a sort of 19th Century regimen of discipline; they don't care whether anything I write makes a nickel, they want to lick me into some kind of seriousness toward my talents, which of course will destroy anything amiable in my character, but will set me on the road to a career of sorts. . . . Aside from the et ceteras of gratefulness and astonishment I feel about this proposition, I have a horrible feeling that this will be the making of me, that it will be good-bye to the joys of messing about. So for the coming year I have laid in 3 pairs of Bermuda shorts, since I shall rarely emerge from 1539 York Avenue.

With the freedom to write full-time, Nelle began dropping off batches of pages at Crain's office. Crain gave her notes, which she incorporated into *Go Set a Watchman*. He did not like the title, so she changed it to *Atticus*. When Crain felt it was ready, he sent the manuscript to the publisher J. B. Lippincott. The Lippincott editors were interested. By the time Nelle received this news, she had already turned in over one hundred pages to Crain for another novel called *The Long Goodbye*, but her focus shifted when Crain told her that she had her first editorial meeting to discuss *Atticus* scheduled at a publishing house.

Tay Hohoff, who was to become Nelle's beloved editor, described their first meeting this way: "On a hot day in June, 1957, a dark-haired, dark-eyed young woman walked shyly into our office on Fifth Avenue to meet most of our editorial staff. They were all men, except me, and apparently we looked formidable. Harper Lee has since admitted she was terrified."

The meeting focused on *Atticus*, which Tay described as full of life. "It was real. The people walked solidly on the pages; they could be seen and heard and felt." But the editors at Lippincott wanted to know if Nelle would be willing to do major revisions. At this point, they said it was "more of a series of anecdotes than a fully conceived novel." Nelle's answer was a simple, "Yes sir, yes ma'am. I'll try."

The editors wished her luck, but they did not offer her a contract.

Nelle worked all summer on *Atticus* and turned in the manuscript again. There were still problems, but it was clear that Nelle was able to take criticism and do the work necessary to bring the book to life. Lippincott offered a contract in October for "an advance of a few thousand dollars." The relationship that Nelle shared with Tay Hohoff was remarkably different from what most editors and authors share nowadays. Nelle and Tay spent a very close two and a half years working together on the novel. Describing the process, Tay said Nelle was relieved to learn that an editor's "teeth were made more for talking with than biting," and the two of them became close friends. Tay nurtured Nelle and encouraged her through each draft to go deeper into the material. She later wrote that she discovered in Nelle "a vivid and original personality hiding behind her intense reserve," and she found that offering even a suggestion was enough to get her off and running.

Still, there were also days when writing a novel seemed absolutely insurmountable for Nelle. It was "like building a house with matches." Did the threads hold together? Was there a plot? Did the characters seem believable? What was she doing even trying to write a novel? Would her efforts ever amount to anything?

One night, her frustration with the revisions mounted into a full-blown panic. Nelle could quite possibly let down everybody who believed in her—

her agent, Maurice Crain, Tay Hohoff, the Browns, and her English teacher, Mrs. Gladys Watson Burkett, who'd even read drafts of the manuscript when Nelle was home in Alabama. And then there was Truman, who'd encouraged her to move to New York in the first place. . . . Maybe Alice and her father were right about her staying in Alabama. Self-doubt and fear raced through her mind. Suddenly, Nelle wanted to quit. What was the point?

Her heart was pounding. It felt as if she'd been in that tiny cold-water flat forever. She couldn't see her way to the end of her book and could hardly stand to look at it another second. In a fit of rage, she tore the last sheet out of the typewriter, opened her window, and threw the entire manuscript out into the snow, watching the pages swirl through the air like giant snowflakes. Immediately, Nelle panicked and called Tay to tell her what she'd done—how two years of work was getting soaked with New York snow.

Tay told her with great calm to go outside and pick up those pages. Now. Tay had invested too much time and energy in Nelle and her book not see it through. In the frigid winter night, Nelle gathered up the pages and brought them inside to dry. From that point on, she made up her mind to finish, no matter what it took. She owed at least that much to her editor, whom she adored, and who believed in her.

In late spring of 1959, Nelle turned in the final draft of what was now called *To Kill a Mockingbird* to Tay Hohoff. The two had worked three years together on the book. Tay later wrote about her time with Nelle from the beginning:

> There were dangling threads of plot, there was a lack of unity—a beginning, a middle, an end that was inherent in the beginning. It is an indication of how seriously we were impressed by the author that we signed a contract at that point. The next two and a half years are among my happiest recollection. . . . [T]he book took shape, grew, matured, acquired depths and heights absent from the delightful but incomplete manuscript we had first seen.

The book wouldn't be published until July 1960,

so while it was in the prepublication stages, Nelle had time on her hands to get back to her earlier novel. That same year, 1959, Truman wrote a letter to his aunt, Mary Ida Carter, and said the following: "Yes, it is true that Nelle Lee is publishing a book. I did not see Nelle last winter, but the previous year, she showed me as much of the book as she'd written, and I liked it very much. She has real talent." He also wrote to some of his Hollywood friends, David O. Selznick and Jennifer Jones, about Nelle's book: "On July 11th, Lippincott is publishing a delightful book: TO KILL A MOCKINGBIRD by Harper Lee. Get it. It's going to be a great success. In it, I am the character called 'Dill'—the author being a childhood friend."

Chapter Seven

IN NOVEMBER 1959, Truman asked Nelle for a favor. He wanted her to go with him to a place called Holcomb, Kansas. A family of four had been murdered there on their farm late one night, and he hoped to write the story of how a small town reacts to a brutal crime. He needed her help with research, editing, and making connections with the townspeople.

Nelle had always been fascinated by crime stories, and when Truman invited her to come to Kansas, she said, "It was deep calling to deep." Not only was her curiosity piqued, but she also wanted to help her friend.

It all began on November 16, 1959, when Truman read a story in *The New York Times* with the headline: WEALTHY FARMER, 3 OF FAMILY SLAIN. The story read,

"A wealthy wheat farmer, his wife and their two young children were found shot to death today in their home. They had been killed by shotgun blasts at close range after being bound and gagged."

Truman became obsessed with this horrific crime and wanted to write a piece for *The New Yorker* magazine about murder in small-town America. There were four victims—the parents, Herbert and Bonnie Clutter, and their two teenage children, Nancy and Kenyon. There were no known motives or suspects. Truman decided to go to Kansas to research the story, but he didn't want to go alone. To make it the best possible story, he knew he needed the support of a good friend and an assistant who could help him with the demanding process of interviewing a lot of people. A second pair of eyes and ears would make the story as accurate as possible, which is why he called upon the one person he knew he could trust.

Nelle had worked hard to perfect *To Kill a Mockingbird* but had no idea how the public would react to it. It wouldn't be out until July 1960, and she simply hoped that the critics would be "merciful." She was working on a new book, but it wasn't coming fast, so maybe she thought going away to help Truman might give her a fresh perspective. In December 1959, approximately a month after the murders, the two of them boarded a train headed west to Garden City, Kansas. After three days on the train, Nelle and Truman stood under the Kansas sky, which yawned bleak and wide before them.

Truman had been a well-known author for ten years, and the president of Kansas State University, James McCain, said he would help him with introductions in Holcomb—McCain had even known the Clutter family—if Truman would first agree to speak to the English faculty. The English department hosted a party in his honor. Afterward, they rented a Chevrolet in Manhattan, Kansas, and drove the rest of they way.

They settled in at the Warren Hotel, once called "Waldorf of the Prairies." After they were rested from the trip they set out to meet the people of the town. They began with Alvin Dewey, the lead detective on the case, but Dewey was immediately suspicious of Truman's odd attire. He went to the police station in a sheepskin coat, a long scarf that dragged along the floor, a little cap, and what appeared to be moccasins. He didn't dress or act like the other reporters. Nor did he endear himself to Dewey when he showed up without press credentials and only a passport to offer as identification. Truman nicknamed Dewey "Foxy," because, like a fox, there was no getting around him. Dewey had two words for Nelle and Truman regarding the criminal case files: No access.

It didn't help matters when Truman announced that he didn't care whether the case would ever be solved or not. Dewey had been a friend of the Clutters, and he cared very much about catching the murderers and bringing them to justice. At this point, however, Truman was more interested in the psychological effect of the crime on the small town.

With the murders only weeks old and the criminals still on the loose, the townsfolk were understandably skittish and distrustful of Truman. Besides his falsetto voice, he appeared rather flamboyant to the folks of western Kansas, with one of his trunks packed with cigarettes, food, and wine. Nelle said later, "He was afraid that there wouldn't be anything to eat in Kansas."

Gay men in Kansas in 1959 were basically invisible, and nobody had seen anyone like him before. A few locals speculated that he might even be the murderer.

"It looked as if the case would never be solved," Nelle said. "Everyone was looking at his neighbors, wondering if they could be murderers—the killings seemed so motiveless. You'd see porch lights on all night. We were given the cold shoulder. Those people had never seen anything like Truman—he was like someone coming off the moon."

The opposite was true of Nelle. She was like the girl next door, with her sense of humor and easy ways, which immediately made people feel comfortable in her presence. One of the Kansas Bureau of Investigation agents, Harold Nye, called her "an absolutely fantastic lady. I really liked her very much. But I did not get a very good impression of the little son of a bitch [Truman]. We go up there and he's parading around in his negligee, it was not a good impression . . . and that impression never changed."

Dolores Hope, a *Garden City Telegram* columnist, said, "Nelle walked into the kitchen, and five minutes later I felt like I'd known her for a long time." She knew how to listen and make eye contact, and her whole focus was drawing the attention back to Truman so he could get his story written. Hope also said Nelle behaved a little like a mother to Truman—"almost like you have a child who doesn't behave well."

In those first few weeks, Truman began to feel desperate, though, because he couldn't get the town to trust him or open up in any way. He confided in Nelle, "I cannot get any rapport going with these people. I can't get a handle on them."

She replied, "Hang on. You will penetrate this place."

Garden City wasn't all that different from Monroeville in terms of small-town manners and how men and women behaved. Nelle said "please" and "thank you" and never showed up empty-handed when invited to dinner. She "cast herself in the unlikely role of occasional legal advisor and researcher for Truman, having come within a semester of a law degree at the University of Alabama." Nelle knew how important this book was to him, and acted with absolute profes-

The Clutter family home where the four murders occurred that inspired Truman's In Cold Blood, *1959.*

sionalism. She was there on a "fact-finding" and "mood gathering" mission to help collect the details for his story, serving as his backup at every interview, listening carefully and observing each nuance and gesture. It was also no doubt a relief for her to focus her energy on assisting Truman after spending the past two and a half years on her novel.

Not surprisingly, she was the one who ultimately

broke the ice in Holcomb. Without Nelle, Truman might never have gained access, much less the town's trust. She drew a map to help him remember the geography of the place and provided insight into people and characters. Truman described Nelle to author George Plimpton in these words: "She is a gifted woman, courageous and with a warmth that instantly kindles most people, however suspicious or dour."

Even though no one would speak to Truman and Nelle at first, when Cliff Hope, the Clutters' estate attorney, learned that the two of them would be spending Christmas alone in the hotel, he invited them to Christmas dinner. Alvin Dewey and his wife, Marie, were there, too, which gave Truman and Nelle a chance to make a new impression on the detective. Truman charmed the dinner party with tales of famous movie stars he knew. In the end both Truman and Nelle became very close to the Deweys, and their friendship lasted for years. After Christmas, invitations began to flood in, and Truman and Nelle's days became packed with interviews. Suddenly, people were willing to talk about the murders.

During the interviews, neither Nelle nor Truman ever took a single note. They wanted people to feel comfortable and open up, and Truman felt that taking notes affected the atmosphere. He believed that people would talk more about themselves if the interviews felt like ordinary conversations. Truman had studied the Sears & Roebuck catalog to improve his memory, and he claimed to have trained himself to remember conversations with up to 90 percent accuracy. When he and Nelle couldn't remember something a person said, they did another interview and posed their questions in a new way. They even interviewed the same people three times in a row to make sure they had it right.

On December 30, 1959, Las Vegas policemen arrested two suspects in the Clutter case, Perry Smith, twenty-nine, and Dick Hickock, twenty-eight, which changed the course of Truman's entire project. Initially, his story was going to be a piece for *The New Yorker*, but now that two suspects had been apprehended, Truman realized he wanted a much longer story. He couldn't possibly say all he wanted to say in an article. It had to be a book, a new kind of book—"a nonfiction novel" is what he called it. "I had this theory about reportage," Capote told *Newsweek* magazine in 1966 about what would become his book *In Cold Blood*. "I've always felt that if you brought the art of the novelist together with the technique of journalism—fiction with the added knowledge that it was true—it would have the most depth and impact."

Nelle was right there helping him every step of the way those first few months in Kansas. They had already done most of the reporting, but now he needed to learn the story of the murderers. Why did they do it? Smith and Hickock had heard a rumor from another ex-con that Herb Clutter had a safe with thousands of dollars in it. They decided to go to the farm, get the money, and kill all witnesses. When they arrived they found no safe or money, but they killed the family anyway. In the days after it was over, the two murderers went on a crime spree, writing bad checks all the way to Las Vegas.

Nelle wound up typing 150 singled-spaced pages of notes for *In Cold Blood*. They are included in Truman's papers, which are kept at the New York Public Library. Truman dedicated the book to her, but it took another six years before it was finished. He couldn't publish the book without knowing the fate of Smith and Hickock.

Some in Holcomb didn't like the way Truman depicted them in his book. Myrt Clare, an ex-postmistress, said, "I thought it was all right but some people around Holcomb had fits. They felt it was described as a broken-down place with hicks, but that's the way it is, and if the shoe fits wear it, that's what I say."

It should be noted that Truman was later accused of unethical journalism practices, such as lying to interview subjects and changing or omitting details to serve the story that became *In Cold Blood*. If he'd been writing fiction, it wouldn't have mattered, but he wasn't. One critic wrote, "For Capote, the end justified his unscrupulous means, and he surely sent a message to some aspiring journalists over the years."

By the winter of 1960, it was time for Nelle to go back to New York. She made a few more trips to Kansas with Truman to watch the court proceedings involving Hickock and Perry, who were facing the death penalty and were ultimately sentenced to death by hanging. But *In Cold Blood* was Truman's book. It always had been.

Nelle the year after the publication of To Kill a Mockingbird, *1961.*

Chapter Eight

NELLE NEEDED TO focus on writing her new novel as well as get ready for the publication of *To Kill a Mockingbird,* which was coming out in July. The pre-publication buzz was already generating a lot of excitement in New York, with early reviews glowing with praise.

Although she never dreamed it at the time, Nelle's months with Truman in Kansas were in a way the last real "normal" period in her life. No longer would she be just Truman's childhood friend/research assistant or A. C. Lee's daughter or Miss Alice Lee's little sister living up in New York City. The millions of people on the verge of hearing about her for the first time would never even know her name was Nelle. She was about to become Harper Lee.

On July 11, 1960, *To Kill a Mockingbird* was published, and Nelle's agents, Maurice Crain and Annie Laurie Williams, threw her a party. A sheet cake decorated with an exact replica of the book jacket was served, and Nelle cut the first piece. The gathering was a lovely celebration for this first-time novelist.

Truman had given her a book jacket quote, which read: "Someone rare has written this very fine first novel: a writer with the liveliest sense of life and the warmest, most authentic humor. A touching book; and so funny, so likeable."

Nelle was hoping for a little encouragement from the critics, and Tay Hohoff had warned her that her book might sell only two thousand copies, which was typical for a first novel. Instead, it hit the *New York Times* best-seller list, where it stayed for eighty-eight weeks. F. H. Lyell of the *Times* wrote, "The dialogue of Miss Lee's refreshingly varied characters is a constant delight in its authenticity." *The New Yorker* said, "Miss Lee is a skilled and totally unpretentious writer who slides unconcernedly and irresistibly back and forth between being sentimental, tough, melodramatic, acute, and funny in this story." *San Francisco Chronicle* writer

George McMichael wrote, "The novel is a moving plea for tolerance." Richard Sullivan of the *Chicago Tribune* wrote, "So admirably done that it must be called both honorable and engrossing, of rare excellence."

Not all reviews were glowing. *Booklist* called it "melodramatic," and the *Atlantic* said the book was "frankly and completely impossible, being told in the first person by a six-year-old with the prose of a well-educated adult."

But negative reviews were definitely in the minority. Tay wrote an essay for the Literary Guild, which stated that the time she spent working with Harper Lee on *To Kill a Mockingbird* was the happiest years of her life, and she was thrilled to help usher this book into the world.

Harper Lee has been writing from her small childhood, but she has never been published before. I mention this particularly because too many young writers try for publication before they are ready—and try with material that is alien to them for one or another reason. Harper Lee, with unerring perception, drew on the life she knew best, the world of her youth, the people who made that world, and the place—the South—that had held the history of her family for generations.

Tay's essay continues, "The old legends about the poets who turn out their villanelles while starving in attics came perilously close to fact in her case."

Frances Nettles, a *Monroe Journal* columnist who covered the book's publication, was clearly suspicious of Tay's interpretation of Nelle's life as a starving artist, wryly noting: "Impressive information, but we know Alice and Mr. Lee too well to recognize it as completely factual. And, besides, Nelle looked healthy enough on a recent trip South from her adopted homestead, New York City."

The bookseller of Monroeville, Ernestine Hardin of Ernestine's Gift Shop, was rumored to have ordered one hundred copies for the premiere book signing. Monroevillians were scandalized at the large number of books—they thought Hardin was at risk of being left with a huge number of unsold copies. A. C. Lee agreed, and out of concern for the bookseller, told Miss

Ernestine that he would buy whatever copies were left over.

All that summer and fall, fan mail arrived in huge sacks at J. P. Lippincott, most of it praising Nelle, although one terse letter said: "In this day of mass rape of white women who are not morons, why is it that you young Jewish authors seek to whitewash the situation." Nelle later said she wished to reply, "Dear Sir or Madam, somebody is using your name to write dirty letters. You should notify the F.B.I." Mostly, she tried to answer every letter and follow through on all her engagements, but it was overwhelming to keep up with the barrage of people requesting interviews to learn more about this young woman from Alabama.

In an interview for the *Birmingham Post Herald*, Nelle described *To Kill a Mockingbird* in her own words:

"My book has a universal theme," Nelle said, "it's not a 'racial' novel. It portrays an aspect of civilization. I tried to show the conflict of the human soul— reduced to its simplest terms. It's a novel of man's conscience . . . universal in the sense it could happen to anybody, anywhere people live together. Take out or substitute any of several factors and you would still have the same question. What makes human beings act as they do?"

In the same interview, Nelle continued, "It amuses me that 'Mockingbird' is taken as a dreadfully liberal novel by some of our dinosaurs. It's not liberal or conservative. I just hope it's a good book. I've had many communications from people in small towns who identify themselves with characters in 'Mockingbird' . . . But you know no one yet has identified any two characters with the same person."

But a *Monroe Journal* article reported, "Although publishers have avowed the Lee novel is not autobiographical and resemblance to 'real' people is coincidental, Monroevillians who read the book will see familiar names. Some events and situations are tinged with local color." This was true of the Boulware family, who threatened to sue for defamation of character for Nelle's depiction of Boo Radley, but they chose not to pursue it.

Nelle had a signing at Capitol Books in Montgomery, Alabama, that was attended by many friends from the University of Alabama. Her father accompanied her, but he was eighty-one and rather frail by then. He'd lost weight and looked tired, but his pride in Nelle was evident. He said in an interview, "I never dreamed of what was going to happen. It was somewhat of a surprise, and it's very rare indeed when a thing like this happens to a country girl going to New York. She will really have to do a good job next time if she goes on up." Mr. Lee continued, "I feel what I think a justifiable measure of pride in her accomplishment, and I must say she had displayed much determination, confidence and ambition to give up a good job in New York and take a chance at writing a book. I'm very proud to be the father of Nelle, and although she has been inclined to writing since childhood, I am simply amazed that this thing should happen to her."

Nelle once said of her father, "It was also typical of him that he did not see himself in the book at all. He was surprised when people greeted him on the street with, 'Hello, Atticus,' but eventually, he began signing the book 'Atticus.'"

There were more book signings, interviews, and new reviews coming out every day. It seemed there was always something else for Nelle to do. In a letter from Truman to Marie and Alvin Dewey three months after the publication of *To Kill a Mockingbird*, he wrote: "Had a note from Nelle—who is now 'hiding out' in Connecticut. Poor thing—she is nearly demented: says she gave up trying to answer her 'fan mail' when she received 62 letters in one day. I wish she could relax and enjoy it more: in this profession it's a long walk between drinks."

By August of 1960, *To Kill a Mockingbird* was on the *New York Times* and *Chicago Tribune* top ten bestseller lists. By September, *To Kill a Mockingbird* was selling more than ten thousand copies weekly. The book was picked as a Literary Guild Selection, Book-of-the-Month Club Alternate, Reader's Digest Condensed Book, and British Book Society Choice. Very few first novels get even one of those honors, much less all of them at once. By early 1961, it had already sold two and a half million copies. That same year, it won the National Book Award and the Pulitzer Prize for the best American novel of 1960, the most distinguished honor for a work of American fiction.

When *To Kill a Mockingbird* won the Pulitzer Prize,

the phone really rang off the hook in Monroeville, and both Alice and A. C. answered calls from people who wanted to talk about the book and Harper Lee. Fans were already asking when the next book was coming out. Alice told one reporter, "I talked with Nelle twice in New York. She has been so busy with things concerning this novel that she hasn't had time to start another one. I know she would like to, but she simply hasn't had time." This wasn't exactly accurate. Nelle was presumably one hundred pages into *The Long Goodbye*, but there wasn't time to work on it.

Nelle went home to Monroeville for the winter of 1961 and often slipped out to the golf course to get a break from the invitations and demands that only seemed to be increasing every day. Alice needed her at home because their father's health was becoming more fragile. And there was also less pressure on Nelle in Monroeville than in New York.

The golf course was the one place where Nelle could think about story plots without interruption. She began to golf more than ever in order to plot her next novel, because of all the visitors who dropped by anytime in Monroeville. In an interview with a Cleveland newspaper, Nelle explained: "'I've found I can't write on my home grounds,' she said. 'I have about 300 personal friends who keep dropping in for a cup of coffee. I've tried getting up 6:00, but then all the 6 o'clock risers congregate. But I'm not getting much done here, either, so I'm going some place else—I won't say where.'"

She told another reporter, "I am more of a rewriter than a writer. I write at least three drafts. I've been writing since I was a kid of seven. But I have systematically thrown out most of what I have written. It was a form of self-training. Playing golf is the best way I know how to be alone and still be doing something. You hit the ball, think, and take a walk. I do my thinking walking. I do my dialog, talking it out to myself."

Nelle called herself the "luckiest woman in the world," and she could hardly believe that her first novel was continuing to generate so much press and excitement. But the book had struck a nerve in the country and around the world. *To Kill a Mockingbird* became a kind of symbol of the civil rights movement, and it opened the door for people to discuss race relations in a new way. Retired English teacher and Monroeville native Mary Tucker said "it told the truth" even if some didn't want to hear it. Tucker, the mother of 2007 Pulitzer journalist Cynthia Tucker, said that once a student asked if she herself ever wanted to be white, and she said, "I never wanted to be white. I just wanted the same opportunities whites had." Another Monroeville native and author, Mark Childress, said, "*To Kill a Mockingbird* had a lot to do with that [racial climate] in the same way that *Uncle Tom's Cabin* woke people up to injustice 100 years earlier."

Nelle was asked if *To Kill a Mockingbird* was an indictment against a group in society, that is, was she denouncing white people for their treatment of blacks during the twentieth century. She replied: "This book is not an indictment so much as a plea for something, a reminder to people at home. . . . [In] the book I tried to give a sense of proportion to life in the South, that there isn't a lynching before every breakfast. I think Southerners react with the same kind of horror as other people do about the injustice in their land."

✳   ✳   ✳

On a more personal level, as a new author, Nelle was simply grateful for the book's success. It meant that even with all her self-doubt and worries, she had made the right choice when she moved to New York in 1949. But it was also slowly dawning on her that such massive success came with a price. She was now a public figure, expected to give interviews and make appearances at a steady clip. Nelle would never feel comfortable giving speeches and holding court. Still, she kept her sense of humor and could be very funny in interviews. When one reporter asked, "How did the lawyers you know like the book?" Nelle answered, "Southern lawyers don't read novels much."

The same reporter asked, "What's the premise of your new book?" and she replied, "That's a large question for so early in the morning."

He wanted to know if people presumed that "the name 'Harper Lee' belongs to a man." Nelle said, "Yes. Recently, I received an invitation to speak at Yale University and was told I could stay in the men's dormitory. But I declined that part of the invitation." Then she smiled and added, "With reluctance."

In an interview with the *Christian Science Monitor*,

Nelle said, "'I cling to old gentlemen like Charles Lamb and Robert Louis Stevenson,' with an appreciative murmur, 'to Jane Austen, writing, cameo-like, in that little corner of the world of hers and making it universal.' Miss Lee also likes Thomas Love Peacock, 'a male Jane Austen,' and the memoirs of nineteenth-century English clergymen."

One of Nelle's classmates, Anne Hines Farish, said, "We had a party for Nelle when her book came out not dreaming it would be anything. She was a tomboy with a dry wit and a wonderful sense of humor. She was just like we were . . . but later, when Gregory Peck came to town? Well, that changed things. Considerably."

With sales booming for what Nelle and Alice began to refer to as "The Bird," Hollywood had come calling.

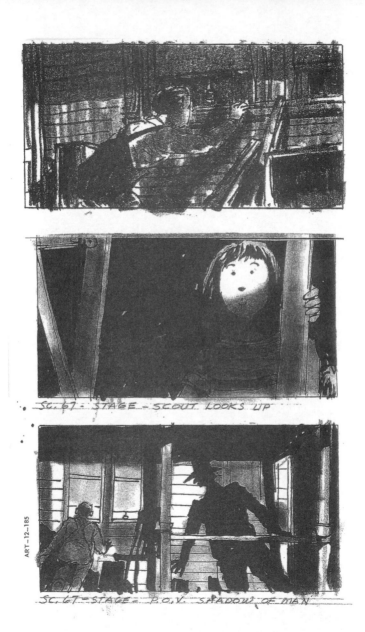

SC. 67 - STAGE - SCOUT LOOKS UP

SC. 67 - STAGE - P.O.V. SHADOW OF MAN

Chapter Nine

ANNIE LAURIE WILLIAMS, Nelle's film agent, was the one fielding the calls from Hollywood. The movie industry had noted the tremendous reviews and book sales, and Williams read the proposals from filmmakers wanting to make the book into a movie. Several directors suggested using big-name stars for the major roles. But Williams was protective of Nelle and the book, and she wasn't about to make a hurried decision. The names of all kinds of famous actors were being tossed about to play the role of Atticus, including Gary Cooper, John Huston, Bing Crosby, and Rock Hudson. At first, Nelle thought Spencer Tracy would make the best Atticus.

But the smaller production companies were the

Storyboard of Boo Radley's house by Henry Bumstead for the movie To Kill a Mockingbird, *1962.*

ones most interested in optioning the book for a film. Most prominent Hollywood studios didn't think the book would make a good film. There was no love story and no violence—except for what happened offscreen. The plot also seemed too episodic and almost leisurely in the way it unfolded. Producers were also wary of having a child's point of view carry the film.

Isabel Halliburton, a young woman whose job was to read and recommend books for movie adaptations, gave a copy of *To Kill a Mockingbird* to Alan Pakula, a producer, who read it and sent it to Bob Mulligan, a director. Pakula thought Mulligan would make a great director for the film, because he'd heard such high praise from actors who'd worked with Mulligan in the past. Mulligan was considered "an actor's director."

Pakula also had a meeting with Nelle and her agent in the fall of 1960. During that meeting, Williams stressed the importance of treating this movie with great care. She even wrote Pakula a follow-up letter that said, "From the very beginning, everybody who had anything to do with the book had felt it was *special*, deserving the most thoughtful handling."

In the process of her decision making, Williams also knew that Alice and A. C. Lee would have to give their final approval on who bought the film rights. She thought Pakula and Mulligan would be a good fit because they were decent and trustworthy and weren't about to make a film of bumbling Southern stereotypes. The entire Lee family would need to feel confident that the filmmakers had integrity and sensitivity. In other words, Williams wasn't hawking "M'Bird" to the highest bidder to make a fast buck. She went with the filmmakers whom she felt would do right by Nelle's story.

In the 2005 Universal Legacy series DVD edition of *To Kill a Mockingbird*, Mulligan and Pakula provided voice-over commentary, discussing each scene. They touched on everything from the actors' motivations to the set descriptions to Elmer Bernstein's musical score to how they got child actors into character by treating the movie set like a gigantic playground and never doing more than one or two takes. They agreed that if Halliburton had not recommended the book, it is unlikely the film would have ever been made. Timing was everything. Halliburton's name appeared in the film credits as "assistant to the producer," but she was not cited for bringing the book to the attention of Pakula and Mulligan in the first place.

Keeping Nelle's business affairs in order became critical to the Lee family, who continued to be astonished at the enormous financial success of *To Kill a Mockingbird*. Alice was the businesswoman of the family. She handled people's taxes, wills, and real estate transactions in Monroeville, and continues to do so today. So it was natural that Alice would take over Nelle's affairs when money from the book began to pour in. Neither Alice nor A. C. believed that all this good fortune could last, so they wanted to be frugal with the money. Nelle had no idea how much she had, and there were too many demands on her time for her to manage her own money.

After the film deal was made, Nelle and Alice received a letter from Williams in the winter of 1961 addressed to both of them in Monroeville, which explained:

The sale is to Alan Pakula and Robert Mulligan, who are forming their own production company to produce together, with Bob Mulligan also directing. This is the real "prize" having him direct the Mockingbird picture. Alan is a good producer but he knew when he first talked to Nelle in our office, that he must have a sensitive director to work with him. We think that Bob Mulligan is just right for this picture.

Mulligan and Pakula believed the key to the film was exploring the mysterious world of childhood. They thought being written from the point of view of children was what made Nelle's novel brilliant, and that quality needed to be captured on-screen. When asked, Nelle said she had no interest in writing the screenplay, as she was at work on her second novel. So Mulligan and Pakula found another Southern author, Horton Foote, who would be just right to understand the film's sensibilities. Approximately ten years older than Nelle, Foote was also from a small Southern town, and he was familiar with the manners, rituals, and customs of that particular world.

Foote did not immediately accept the screenwriting offer, though. "I was close friends with Alan Pakula and Bob Mulligan," he said. "They were asking me to adapt the book. I was wanting to write something of my own. Then my wife read the book and she said to me, 'You'd better read that book!'"

Pakula brought Nelle to meet Horton Foote at his

home in Nyack, New York, one evening, and Foote said it was as if they became "instant cousins." She said to him, "I don't want to see you again until you do it."

Foote's greatest dilemma was that the novel stretched out over three years, and he wanted to hone the action of the book into a single year for the screenplay. "I couldn't find an easy way to get into the material. But I discovered a critic who wrote an essay called 'Scout in the Wilderness,' which was about Scout as Huckleberry Finn. Well, that freed me—I thought of Scout as Huckleberry Finn—and it helped me tremendously." Foote's eyes lit up discussing the next-door character of Dill, saying, "The minute that Harper told me that it was Truman as a little boy my imagination went wild."

The film's art director, Henry Bumstead, decided that he needed to take a trip to Monroeville to study the town in order to create the right tone for the film. Nelle met him there to show him the sights, and afterward, he wrote a letter to Pakula describing his visit. Bumstead won an Oscar for his set designs of the film. He donated the following letter, written in November 1961, and all his film storyboards to the Old County Courthouse Museum in Monroeville before his death in 2006.

Dear Alan,

I arrived here in Monroeville this afternoon after a very interesting and beautiful drive from Montgomery. Although this is my first visit to Alabama, I have worked in the South a number of times. During my drive I was very much impressed by the lack of traffic, the beautiful countryside, and the character of the negro shacks that dot the terrain. Harper Lee was there to meet me, and she is a most charming person. She insisted I called her Nelle—feel like I've known her for years. Little wonder she was able to write such a successful novel.

Monroeville is a beautiful little town of about 2500 inhabitants. It's small in size, but large in southern character. I'm so happy you made it possible for me to research the area before designing To Kill a Mockingbird. *Most of the houses are of wood, one story, and set up on brick piles. Almost every house has a porch and a swing hanging from the rafters. Believe me, it's a much more relaxed life than we live in Hollywood.*

So far I have seen all the types of buildings we need for our residential street, but they are scattered throughout the town, so it would have been impossible for us to shoot the picture here in Monroeville. Therefore, I feel that the freeway houses we purchased for our southern street, with sufficient remodeling, will better suit our purposes. I have also photographed a wonderful Boo Radley home, which we can duplicate on our street.

I have also visited the old courthouse square and the interior of the courtroom Nelle wrote about. I can't tell you how thrilled I am by the architecture and the little touches that will add to our sets. Old pot bellied stoves still heat the courtroom and beside each one stands a tub filled with coal. Nelle says we should have a block of ice on the exterior of the courthouse steps when we shoot this sequence. It seems the people chip off a piece of ice to take into the courtroom with them to munch on to try and keep cool. It reminded me of my "youth" when I used to follow the wagon to get ice chips.

Nelle is really amused at my picture taking, and also my taking measurements so that I can duplicate the things I see. She says she didn't know we worked so hard. This morning she greeted me with, "I lost five pounds yesterday following you around taking pictures of door knobs, houses, wagons, collards etc. Can we take time for lunch today?"

The way people look at me around town they must think I'm a Hollywood producer rather than an art director. Nelle warned me about this—that they knew someone from Hollywood was in town, but they didn't know who I was or what I did.

Yesterday afternoon the news was around town that that man from Hollywood was taking pictures in Mrs. Skinner's collard patch. They couldn't understand it because the opinion is that there are much better collard patches around town than Mrs. Skinner's. It seems that after giving me permission to photograph her collards she rushed to the phone to give out the news. I must admit that when I confessed that I'd never seen a collard, both Mrs. Skinner and her colored help looked at me with raised eyebrows.

Nelle says the exterior of Mrs. Dubose's house should have paint that is peeling. Also, the interior should have dark woodwork, Victorian furniture, and be grim. Her house would be wired for electricity, but she would still be using oil lamps—to save money, so Nelle says. Boo Radley's house should look like it had never been painted—almost haunted.

Other items will be useful—the streets should be dirt, and there are no lamp posts as we know them today. The lamps hung from telephone poles. Also, in 1932 they were still using wooden stoves for their cooking and heating.

The almond trees that line some of the streets are beautiful, but I felt we can get the same character by using white oaks. There are no mailboxes on the houses—seems people go to town to the main post office to pick up their mail.

We photographed some negro shacks, which will be of great help when we come to do the exterior of Tom Robinson's shack. Many of the shacks are located in areas covered with pine trees so we could do this sequence on the upper Lake section of the lot where we have pine trees. We also photographed some back porches that will come in handy when we do the back of Boo Radley's. All in all, certainly feel this trip will be of tremendous help in the designing of the picture. Again, my thanks to you. Warmest regards,

Sincerely,

Henry Bumstead

Pakula and Mulligan had decided they wanted actor

Gregory Peck to play Atticus, so they sent him the book, which Peck read in one night. He called the very next day and said, "If you want me I'm your boy." Peck had played the leading man in a great many Hollywood films, including: *The Yearling, Roman Holiday, Moby Dick, Cape Fear, A Gentleman's Agreement*, and *How the West Was Won*. But the role of Atticus Finch would become his favorite part of all.

In January 1962, Peck visited Monroeville to soak up local color and see the town. He also wanted to do some research and meet with Nelle and A. C. While Bumstead's visit had sparked curiosity, Peck's threw the town into a tailspin. The famous actor was spotted all over Monroeville, from the Wee Diner on Pineville Road to the La Salle Hotel to a local bank where a clerk refused to cash Peck's check because he had no identification on him. A manager intervened on his behalf.

It was just fine for a hometown girl to write a pretty good novel, but for Gregory Peck to visit? Now, that was big news! High school girls went out driving to try to find where the handsome movie star was staying.

One girl, Martha Louise Jones Moorer, got lucky and met him:

> We checked the local hotel and found out that they had left, so since there was only one other we tried it. We recognized cars I suppose . . . anyway we decided which room they had to be in so one of the gals dared me to knock on the door and get Mr. Peck's autograph. I did and Nelle answered the door, not even hello, but "Martha Louise, *what* are *you* doing here?" I timidly said I just wanted his autograph. Nelle was just about to slam the door in my face, but he was sitting just inside the door and said he would be happy to give me his autograph. I still have it!

It came time to shoot the film in 1962. Nelle had never been to Hollywood before, but she traveled by train to California to watch the first few weeks of filming.

During her trip west, Nelle told a reporter, "I know authors are supposed to knock Hollywood and complain about how their words are treated here, but I just can't manage it. Everybody has been so darn nice to

Nelle and Gregory Peck dining at the Wee Diner in Monroeville, Alabama, 1962.

me and everything is being done with such care that I can't find anything to complain about."

But she was concerned about Gregory Peck playing Atticus. She wasn't sure if he was right for the part. She'd only seen him play the handsome leading man in films and had met him only the one time when he visited Monroeville. He was lovely and gracious, as was his wife, Veronique Peck, but Nelle was still unconvinced. But when Peck stepped out of his dressing room that morning on the set, she realized that she needn't have worried. Instead of the star she'd come to know on the big screen, a middle-aged man in glasses appeared. He wore a 1933-era suit with a vest and a watch and chain. He did not have on any makeup. Gregory Peck had become Atticus Finch.

As the cameras followed the actors during the first scene on the shooting schedule, Nelle tagged along, watching the action. It was uncanny how much even the California houses looked liked her neighborhood on South Alabama Avenue in the 1930s. A neighborhood of Great Depression houses had been earmarked for demolition in order to build Dodger Stadium. Instead, Bumstead had the homes moved to the set of *To Kill a Mockingbird*. The shutters and the gliders looked so inviting that Nelle wanted to sit down in a rocking chair on a porch and fan herself.

In fact, every detail of the movie town was so real that when the film was released, some filmmakers contacted Pakula and Mulligan to find out where it was shot, so they could shoot their movies in the same place. Other folks claimed, "I know exactly where you filmed it. I've been to that town." Pakula and Mulligan had to explain that the town was just a back lot in Hollywood, and most people didn't believe them.

As Nelle watched Peck strolling down the street in "Maycomb" with the children, tears filled her eyes. Phillip Alford, who played the boy Jem, grabbed his father's briefcase to carry, and they stopped to talk to cranky old Mrs. Dubose. The character of Mrs. Dubose was probably inspired by Nelle's old neighbor Mrs. Jones, who used to yell at Nelle to get cleaned up and out of those overalls.

When the shoot was over, Mulligan said, "Wonderful. First take. It's a print. That scene will be in the movie just the way it is."

Peck, noticing a tear on her cheek, walked over to Nelle. He was feeling "pretty puffed up" and enthused about how well the very first take had gone. He was also curious about her reaction. "Harper, did I see something a little shiny on your check?"

Instead of gushing about his brilliant performance, Nelle, always direct, said, "Oh Gregory, you've got a little potbelly just like my daddy." Peck looked a little surprised, but replied, "Harper, that's great acting!"

Nelle stayed out in Hollywood for three weeks but decided the filmmakers knew what they were doing and went back to New York. She wanted to try to get back to a normal life and routine, but that would not happen anytime soon. She was back home in New York approximately a week after her trip to California when she was called home to Monroeville. Her father, A. C. Lee, had died of a heart attack on Palm Sunday. It was April 15, 1962.

Of her beloved father, Nelle once said, "My father is one of the few men I've known who has genuine humility and it lends him a natural dignity. He has absolutely no ego drive, and so he is one of the most beloved men in this part of the state."

His obituary read: "Lee, a great man and a beloved citizen, contributed significantly to the growth and development of Monroeville."

Before the death of A. C., Peck explained how he felt about the role of Atticus Finch. "I have tried it both ways and have decided to stick to roles I admire. I once played a murderer and decided that kind of role was not for me. I admire Atticus Finch, the character I will portray in *To Kill a Mockingbird* and am delighted to be able to play this part. Mr. Lee is a beautiful man."

A. C. liked Peck, too, although he admitted that he'd never seen any of his movies. After his death, Nelle gave her father's pocket watch to Peck as a gift and a way of saying thank you. The two became lifelong friends.

To honor the memory of A. C., Nelle's publisher, J. B. Lippincott Company, donated three hundred books to the Monroe County Library. Inside each book an inscription read, "Given in memory of A. C. Lee to the Monroe County Library."

After his death, Nelle spent a lot of time with Alice in Monroeville, working on her second novel, said to be set in the South. Their other sister, Louise, was bringing up two boys in Eufaula, Alabama, and their sister-in-law, Sara Ann, was raising their late brother's children, but she had remarried and moved away. Both Nelle and Alice adored the children and no doubt took much comfort in them after the loss of their beloved father.

When the shooting of *To Kill a Mockingbird* wrapped

in June 1962 and the film was being edited, Foote said, "Universal hated the film—they wouldn't admit that now, of course, but they wanted to cut it ten different ways. It was Gregory Peck who saved the film because in his contract he gave Alan and Bob the power to have the final cut. The studio couldn't mess with it. The studio was very nervous—and who knows why studios get nervous? But Gregory Peck saved it and guarded it. He also took a real risk. He was a leading man at the time, and then he was playing a character in glasses. It was a real risk, but he had that commercial star power."

It was a big deal for a handsome star to play a role that required glasses. Leading Hollywood heroes did not wear glasses. Clark Kent wore glasses, but not Superman. Universal Studios kept calling up Pakula after viewing the dailies of scenes to express concern that "Greg Peck" did not appear glamorous and was looking rather old. Should something be done? Pakula chose not to share these concerns with Mulligan because he felt that once a director was on the set, it was his set. "Beware of your need to be needed as a producer, and know when to stand back and shut up" was Pakula's philosophy.

The film premiered in Hollywood around Christmas 1962, in order to make it eligible for the 1963 Academy Awards. But the Southern premiere took place in Mobile, Alabama, on March 15, because the Monroe Theatre in Monroeville was too small for the crowd. While doing a press junket in Chicago to promote the movie, a reporter asked Nelle, "I understand that Gregory Peck, after seeing his straight dramatic performance in Mockingbird, says he will no longer do romantic leads." Nelle deadpanned, "Maybe he liked himself in glasses."

The young actors Mary Badham and Philip Alford, who played Scout and Jem in the film, called Gregory Peck by the name Atticus until his death in 2003. When Peck was asked before filming started if he minded that the children weren't "stars," he replied, "It does not matter about the children being stars. All children live in a world of make-believe and certainly if they are intelligent, they can make the movie, and I am looking forward to working with them."

The film won three Academy Awards: Best Adapted Screenplay (Horton Foote), Art Direction/Set Decoration (Henry Bumstead), and Best Actor (Gregory

Peck). Nelle, in typical fashion, didn't go to Hollywood for the ceremony. She watched it with Alice and some friends in Monroeville. Peck, upon receiving the Oscar for Best Actor, held Nelle's father's pocket watch up and said, "I had a feeling about Harper Lee when I met that young woman, but I didn't know she would provide the greatest success of my career."

But in a 1963 letter to *The Monroe Journal*, Nelle expressed her concern for those expecting to see her father on the screen.

Dear Editor, Last week's Journal ran a picture of Gregory Peck with a caption noting his resemblance to my late father, among other things.

In fairness to everyone concerned, especially to the Monroeville people who are looking forward to seeing the movie "To Kill a Mockingbird," may I say this: anyone who expects to see a portrayal of my father on the screen will be disappointed, for it was never Mr. Peck's intention to reproduce my father's appearance, mannerisms, speech, or any of his personal characteristics.

People who expect to see a portrayal of the charac-

ter Atticus Finch as conceived in the novel will be greatly rewarded, for Mr. Peck has rendered a masterful performance, springing from his own gifts as an artist. To imply that he used the personal characteristics of anyone simply does not do justice to a great actor. When you see the film and judge for yourself, I think you will agree.

Sincerely yours,
Nelle Harper Lee

Nelle's response to the film was pure pleasure. She was thrilled with the voice-over actress Kim Stanley, who narrated the film but didn't appear in the credits. "They treated it like it was a baby," Nelle said. "They handled it with such care, as if it were a fragile jewel. Kim Stanley volunteered to do the narration at the beginning. And when they finished filming and showed the movie back, it was four and a half hours long."

The reason for the length was partly due to the scenes with Mrs. Dubose, played by the character actress Ruth White, when Jem reads to her as a punishment for whacking the heads off of her camellias. These scenes were eventually cut from the film. "It tore my heart out to lose that sequence with Ruth White," Mulligan said. White was a wonderful actress in her forties who had to spend two or three hours a day getting into makeup and two hours getting out of makeup only to end up in a minute or two of the movie. Her acting was said to be so brilliant, however, that it was the kind of work that would have won her an Academy Award nomination. For years afterward, Mulligan apologized to her for cutting the scenes, but he and Pakula knew it was best for the film.

Where was Truman in all of this? The Deweys received a letter from him in 1963, regarding the film and his disproval of Nelle's involvement with it, but he did not dwell long on the subject, and soon returned to the one closest to his heart (*In Cold Blood*) in the postscript.

> *Dearhearts . . .*
> *I think our friend Nelle will meet me in G.C. (Garden City) However, she is so involved in the publicity for her film (she owns a percentage, that's why; even so, I think*

it's very undignified *for any serious artist to allow them-selves to be exploited in this fashion.)* . . .

Much, much love

T.

P.S. I just sent Part Three of the book to Mr. Shawn last week. He cabled me: "A masterpiece stop A work of art people will be reading two hundred years from today." So see—you're not only going to be famous, but immortal! And that's no joke!

Nelle attending a 2007 concert by Birmingham, Alabama, public schools students.

Chapter Ten

WHEN NELLE WAS asked what advice she would give a young writer just starting out, she said:

Well, the first advice I would give is this: hope for the best and expect nothing. Then you won't be disappointed. You must come to terms with yourself about writing. You must not write "for" something; you must not write with definite hopes of reward. People who write for reward by way of recognition or monetary gain don't know what they're doing. They're in the category of those who write; they are not writers.

In the years following the publication of *To Kill a Mockingbird* in 1960, Nelle did everything she was told to do by her publisher. She gave interviews, responded to fan mail, advised filmmakers. She was a good foot soldier playing the part of the new author.

But by 1964, Nelle had grown weary of answering the same questions over and over. She was also frustrated by journalists getting the facts wrong. It's unclear if there was a single, defining incident or just enough is enough, but she called it quits on all formal interviews by 1964. In the following passage, she talks about her meteoric rise to fame and how it all became much too much:

It was like being hit over the head and knocked cold. You see, I never expected any sort of success with "Mockingbird." I didn't expect the book to sell in the first place. I was hoping for a quick and merciful death at the hands of reviewers, but at the same time I sort of hoped that maybe someone would like it enough to give me encouragement. Public encouragement. I hoped for a little, as I said, but I got rather a whole lot, and in some ways this was just about as frightening as the quick, merciful death I'd expected.

✳ ✳ ✳

She entered a quiet period after 1964, and little was reported about her in the media. She spoke to *Time* magazine about Truman's book *In Cold Blood*, but she would no longer discuss *To Kill a Mockingbird*. When she was in Monroeville, she used to call up her good friend Louise Jones, the wife of George Thomas Jones, to play golf with her.

George Thomas Jones said, "Nelle would call Louise to play golf, and finally my wife said, 'Nelle, I like playing golf with you, and I appreciate that you ask me . . . but why do you always ask me and nobody else?' Nelle said, 'Because you never ask me about the book. Or when I'm going to write another one.' Nelle got a bellyful of that stuff," Jones continued. "Once, she played in a tournament with my wife and a bunch of silly women on the other fairway were waving and calling to her, 'Hey Scout! Hey Scout!'"

Nelle suffered a severe burn in late 1964, and in January 1965 Truman wrote to Perry Smith, who was awaiting execution on death row, about her accident. "Nelle is in the hospital, the result of a serious kitchen accident. She burned herself very badly, especially her right hand. It seems some sort of pan caught fire and exploded—all of that at her home in Alabama." Even the act of holding a pen or typing was impossible for a long while. Her only output during this time was an essay published in *McCall's* magazine called "When Children Discover America," encouraging young people to explore their country.

If more young people traveled with their eyes and minds open and saw this country, they would have a deeper feeling about it. Adventuring across the country is out of style. Whatever happened to working after school in a grocery store to get enough money to hitchhike to California during your vacation? My youngest nephew may be one of the last to do that, and he did when he was fifteen. His parents were terrified, but he got himself to the World's Fair. His mother had thoughtfully sewn a bus ticket into the cuff of his trousers, but he swore he would never use it. He ended up in Chicago and lived on milk and rolls for three days because he didn't have any money.

When he finally got home, he had lost thirty pounds; but he was the happiest boy I had ever seen in my life. He had discovered something of America for himself. It will mean something to him for the rest of his life.

In 1966, President Lyndon B. Johnson invited Nelle to the White House to have dinner. The occasion was meant to celebrate both the book and the film, and also how the book had come to act as a symbol of the civil rights movement. Nelle had written *To Kill a Mockingbird* as the early civil rights movement was gaining momentum in the late 1950s. Her book also inspired generations of students to go into law because of Atticus Finch.

To prepare for the White House dinner, a Monroeville resident said, "Nelle just went into Lazenby's [a Monroeville mercantile company] and got a dress off the rack. They sold feed and seed in the front of the store and dresses in the back. Nelle thought that was good enough for her."

Tay Hohoff was very anxious to have Nelle's second

novel by 1968 in time for the 150th anniversary of J. B. Lippincott Publishers. But it wasn't ready. It is not clear how much Tay saw of the new book, but she and Nelle may have decided together that it was not ready for publication, according to Wayne Greenhaw. That same year, Nelle's adored book agent, Maurice Crain, was diagnosed with cancer. He died in 1970, a loss that surely devastated Nelle. Maurice had been the first one to read her early stories and encouraged her to write the novel. Besides being her agents, he and his wife, Annie Laurie Williams, along with Tay, had become Nelle's dearest friends. Four years after the death of Crain, Tay died. Nelle had adored her editor and was deeply hurt by this loss, too. Although Tay had retired, it is likely that Nelle still shared work with her. Finally, Annie Laurie Williams passed away in 1977 after years of health problems, so three of Nelle's major support beams in both her personal and writing life had vanished. Maybe it was hard for her to write another book without them to give her suggestions and feedback.

Nelle has never published a second novel, but Reverend Thomas Lane Butts, her minister and dear friend, said she still types away on a Royal manual typewriter. "Her letters are like a short story. Her powers of description are extraordinary."

It's possible she has never stopped writing at all but has just not made her writing public.

In 1983, Nelle agreed to give a talk about Albert James Pickett, who wrote *Pickett's History of Alabama*, which had been published in 1851. Her sister Louise had arranged the event, and Nelle was willing to do it as a favor to her. *Pickett's History* was one of her favorite books. Her talk, called "Romance and High Adventure," was part of the Alabama History and Heritage Festival. Mercer University Press later published it in the anthology *Clearings in the Thicket*. Nelle focused on her great love of history, and she included passages on the Creek Indians, slavery, and Pickett's brilliance as an author. It went very well, but Nelle was terrified before taking the stage. She admitted to a friend right before the talk, "It's like an owl at noon. You'll never see me do something like this again." And she didn't.

It is not known how much Nelle saw Truman after

1966, when *In Cold Blood* was published with phenomenal success. Once again, he became the toast of New York City, but, like Nelle, he never published another book. He spent his remaining years struggling to finish books and becoming addicted to drugs and alcohol, which ultimately led to his death in 1984. In his book *Lost Friendships*, Donald Windham wrote that Nelle and Truman had not been in touch for fifteen years prior to his death. But biographer Gerald Clarke wrote: "As far as I know, she and Truman never had a falling out, at least not one so serious that they stopped talking. I do know that he called her on my behalf in the mid-seventies and persuaded her to talk to me. She spoke very fondly of him then—this was about eight years before his death—and I have no reason to think she changed her mind after that. He never mentioned a falling out to me, and I'm certain if there had been one, he would have."

Because Nelle never published another book, some time in the 1970s literary conspiracy theorists began to spread a rumor that Truman had actually ghostwritten *To Kill a Mockingbird*. It was a salacious piece of gossip that he did not deny, which fueled it further.

And it was a rumor that Nelle refused to dignify with a response. One can only imagine the betrayal she must have felt.

Historian Dr. Wayne Flynt believes Truman was jealous of Nelle. "He never won a National Book Award or Pulitzer Prize. Toward the end of his drug-induced haze, he began to drop hints that he was the author." A letter dated July 9, 1959, from Truman to his aunt Mary Ida Carter praising Nelle and her novel finally put the rumor to rest when Mary Ida Carter's son, Big Boy, donated the letter to the Monroe County Heritage Museum in 2006.

"Truman's ego would never have allowed him to keep silent if he had written *To Kill a Mockingbird*," Dr. Flynt said. "He would have proclaimed it in great neon lights."

A CBS newscaster once waited for hours outside the United Methodist Church in Monroeville with a crew, hoping to interview Nelle, who was inside. But she stayed in the church with other members until he gave up and went away. And the late George Plimpton once tried to find her in Monroeville to interview her for a book he was doing about Truman, but she went golfing and avoided all contact with him. Nelle wrote to Plimpton, explaining, "I don't like interviews. I just don't do them."

A local Monroeville doctor, Dr. David Stallworth, said: "I'm always a bit bothered when people describe [Nelle] as reclusive. She is private. She guards her privacy. And there's so much more to her than *To Kill a Mockingbird*. My personal opinion is that she had a choice early on. She could become Nelle Harper Lee, or Harper Lee who wrote *To Kill a Mockingbird*, and become the footnote to the novel. No one likes to be marginalized."

Nelle enjoys talking with the young students she meets every spring in Tuscaloosa, Alabama, for an essay contest. In 2001, with the help of the University of Alabama and the Alabama Academy of Honor, Lee started an annual contest for Alabama high school students to write about how the South has and has not changed since the time of *To Kill a Mockingbird*. A ceremony is held every year in Tuscaloosa, and she has never missed one. She speaks with the winners, but avoids journalists—except for one interview in 2006 with *The New York Times*, in which she agreed to discuss only the students and their essays. She told the reporter, "They always see new things in [the book]. . . . And the way they relate it to their lives now is really quite incredible."

In 2006, the predominantly white Mountain Brook High School and the all-black Fairfield Preparatory High School in Birmingham joined forces to produce a play of *To Kill a Mockingbird*. The project began with the vision of Pat Yates, the Mountain Brook drama teacher, who designed the production. Fairfield Preparatory didn't have a drama program, much less a stage, but when Yates met the Fairfield choral director, Patsy Howze, the two decided to bring these two divergent student bodies together. Filmmaker Sandy Jaffe filmed the rehearsals and interviewed students. She made the play the center of her 2009 documentary *Our Mockingbird*. Student Roman Gladney, who played Tom Robinson, was thrilled to be a part of it, and was even more excited that Nelle came to see the play. "Oh my God, it was like I was meeting the president of the United States," said Gladney. Nelle hugged him and gave him an autograph. Gladney asked Nelle about the Tom Robinson character, and she replied that he was "a man with pride."

Another student in Jaffe's documentary responded to the treatment of race in *To Kill a Mockingbird*. Jaffe said, "The idea of being unjustly accused because of one's race still resonates with young people today. An Arab student from a Boston high school talks about how he identifies with Tom Robinson—describing the terrorist attacks of 2001 when he was unjustly accused of being a terrorist just because his family was from Saudi Arabia."

The Big Read was developed by the National Endowment for the Arts to "revitalize" the idea of reading in America, bringing communities together to read and discuss a single book. *To Kill a Mockingbird* has been one of the most frequently selected "Big Reads" in cities and towns across America. Author Nina Revoyr works with incarcerated men in Los Angeles and helped develop the curriculum for the "Big Read in Corrections" pilot program. In an interview, she noted how all of the prisoners in their twenties identified most strongly with the character of Boo Radley.

"We had a long discussion about whether or not he was really 'crazy,'" Revoyr said. "Their observation was that his situation was the equivalent of being put in isolation. They also noted his attempts to reach out, and drew some parallels. They also noted how Boo's friends had different outcomes—the kid who went to vocational school and ended up as an engineer." This led to discussions of why inmates needed something productive to do while incarcerated.

At the Lifetime Achievement Awards at the Birmingham Pledge Foundation in 2006, Nelle spoke to Nancy Womble, the daughter of one of her childhood friends, Margaret McNeil. Womble sent an e-mail in 2008 describing this chance meeting:

> *After reading the unauthorized biography by Charles Shields, I realized that my Aunt Ruth (Mrs. Leighton McNeil) taught Nelle Lee in first grade. This was mentioned on page 32 of this book. I then began to call the only living relative to ask about mother and her relationship with Ms. Lee.*
>
> *My aunt and uncle in Mobile, Alabama— Charles and Evelyn McNeil told me that my mother and Nelle Lee were childhood friends. Mother*

would play at Nelle's house and Nelle would play at my mother's house. This was something I never heard about since my mom died one month after my 9th birthday, in 1969.

I arrived early that evening—not dreaming that I would see Ms. Lee before the presentation. Not only did I see her, but without hesitation, I approached her and asked her directly if she indeed knew my mother.

Nancy: "My mother was from Frisco City," I blurted out, "but she died when I was 9 years old."

Ms. Lee: "Who was your mother?"

Nancy: "Margaret McNeil."

Ms. Lee: "Who?"

Nancy: "Margaret McNeil."

Ms. Lee, after hearing the name clearly, opened her arms to me and tilted her head in such a gentle and loving way.

Ms. Lee: "Of course I knew your mother. Of course she was my friend. She was a lovely person."

It was a wonderful moment of confirmation and grace for me.

* * *

In a 2007 interview, Angela Roberts, the former librarian at Alabama Southern College in Monroeville, said, "I met Nelle when I started working here, and she'd come by to pick up the Sunday *New York Times* crossword puzzle for Miss Alice. She loves talking to children and young people—she will talk and listen to them for hours, but she has no patience with adults or journalists who only want to ask her nosy questions or pry into her private life. She loves fruitcake, and she and Alice always give away fruitcakes in December." Roberts also described how Nelle used to sign three hundred copies of her book every year to donate to the students at Alabama Southern College. Then a colleague of Roberts's began selling signed copies on eBay for six hundred dollars each. Enraged, Nelle quit signing her books for Alabama Southern and will no longer sign books, except in special circumstances.

George Thomas Jones, a native Monroevillian historian and columnist for the *Monroe Journal*, described one of those special signing circumstances. A family with a teenage son in a coma had a first edition of *To Kill a Mockingbird*. Jones said they had approached him about asking Nelle to sign the first edition, so they could sell it to pay for their son's hospital bills. Jones asked nine of Nelle's friends in Monroeville if they would ask Nelle to sign the book, but all nine people said no. They did not feel comfortable asking her. George didn't approach her himself, because he hadn't been on speaking terms with Nelle and Alice ever since he had published an article Alice had asked him not to run in the *Monroe Journal*. Finally, he wrote to Nelle, "Dear Nelle, I don't give a hoot if you sign the book or not. It's not for me." He explained that it was for the family, and left the note and book at Alice's office. A few hours later, the phone rang. Nelle said, "George, I'll sign the book."

Jones paused in his telling of the story and then grinned. "Small town stuff."

In 2007, Nelle was inducted in the Alabama Academy of Honor and spoke only these words at the ceremony: "It's better to be silent than to be a fool." That same year, in November, the White House awarded Nelle America's highest civilian honor by giving her the Presidential Medal of Freedom for her contribution to the world of literature. She attended the ceremony with Veronique Peck, Gregory's wife, but she did not speak. A White House statement said: "At a critical moment in our history, her beautiful book, *To Kill a Mockingbird*, helped focus the nation on the turbulent struggle for equality."

The redbrick Colonial home where Nelle and Alice currently live is on the same block where Nelle attended high school. The school is now Monroeville Junior High, where ironically a 2008 discrimination lawsuit was filed by the ACLU on behalf of parents of black students who claimed their children were the target of racial slurs and were kept out of AP classes. The lawsuit is ongoing.

When Nelle was a child, church was the town's principal recreation—church picnics, church socials, and football games between the Baptists and Methodists. Even today, seventy-five churches dot Monroe County alone. Alice is very involved in the Methodist Children's Homes in Alabama, including group homes in Dothan and Huntsville.

Every spring the "Mockingbird Players," a group

of local citizens, put on a production of *To Kill a Mockingbird* that brings thousands of visitors to Monroeville. Tickets sell out almost immediately. Act one takes place on the lawn of the County Courthouse. The second act is set inside the courtroom, and jurors (all men) are picked from the audience.

The county commissioner, Charles McCorvey, plays Tom Robinson. "It's 1935 and survival means 'yassuh this and that,' and being mindful and second-class," says McCorvey. "I had a difficult time with the role until I could leave who I really am and realize I am not in the 21st century."

Mel's Dairy Dream, a drive-through ice-cream stand, sits on the lot where Nelle's childhood home used to be on South Alabama Avenue. Next door to Mel's is an empty lot with a stone fence and a historical marker noting Truman Capote's boyhood home. A Conoco Service station stands where the Boulware house used to be in the 1930s. For Heaven's Sakes, the only bookstore in town, closed a few years ago, and it did not carry *To Kill a Mockingbird*.

Nelle does not want a historical marker with her name. When citizens of Monroeville suggested the idea of a "Harper Lee Day" to her, she turned them down flat. She also turned down an offer to appear on *The Oprah Winfrey Show* in 2006 but sent a letter that was published in O magazine. In the letter, she wrote of the comfort of curling up in bed with a book as a child. "Now, 75 years later in an abundant society where people have laptops, cell phones, iPods, and minds like empty rooms, I still plod along with books."

Two recent films about Truman's research and writing of *In Cold Blood*, *Capote* and *Infamous*, depict Nelle's friendship with Truman. Nelle told Wayne Greenhaw, "The first one [actress Catherine Keener] had my name but that was the end of any likeness. And if New York had a party for my premiere they didn't invite me. However, the Capote actor [Philip Seymour Hoffman] got it." As for Sandra Bullock's portrayal of her in *Infamous*, Nelle only said, "I never wore socks."

For many years, Nelle spent most of her time in New York, a city she considered her real home. When there, Nelle loved cheering for the New York Mets, but when company came to town she would suffer through a Yankees game if necessary. A friend said, "New York is truly her home, but she came back [to Monroeville] for Alice." Later, Nelle lived half the year in New York and half in Monroeville, returning to Monroeville each September to celebrate Alice's birthday. Nelle, now in her eighties, and Alice, in her nineties, have spent their senior years together exploring the back roads of lower Alabama. Alice said, "We go out in every nook and cranny. We explore. If a new road opens up, we try it. We have done that all our lives."

Neither sister ever married, but they remain close to their other sister, Louise, and her family. In 1997, Louise said, "I wish she would talk. I'm very proud of her. I'm very proud of my other sister too. In a way, Alice is more remarkable, because she's 86 years old and still a practicing attorney. I'd love to talk about my sister to you, but I know how my sister feels. I don't want to do anything to mar the love we have for each other."

Alice and Nelle are both in frail health, but they keep each other going. Alice is deaf but wears a hearing aid, and Nelle, going deaf, also suffers from macular degeneration, which makes it difficult to read—the thing that gives her the most pleasure. She currently resides full-time in Monroeville due to a stroke she suffered in November 2007. But her health has been improving, and she celebrated her eighty-second birthday quietly with friends who said she was looking frail but feeling better. She was well enough to travel to Birmingham in May 2008 to receive an honorary law degree bestowed on her by the Alabama Bar Association. She was awarded the honor for creating the character of Atticus Finch who "has become the personification of the exemplary lawyer in serving the legal needs of the poor."

In 1964, Nelle told Roy Newquist that all she wanted was to be the Jane Austen of South Alabama. In the same interview, she talked about how much writing meant to her:

> You know, many writers don't like to write . . . I like to write. Sometimes, I'm afraid that I like it too much because when I get into work I don't want to leave it. As a result I'll go for days and days without leaving the house or wherever

I happen to be. I'll go out long enough to get papers and pick up some food and that's it. It's strange, but instead of hating writing, I love it too much.

Her late cousin, Richard "Dickie" Williams, who ran a souvenir gift shop in Monroeville's town square, said, "I asked her one time why she never wrote another book. She told me, 'When you have a hit like that, you can't go anywhere but down.'"

Reliable sources requesting anonymity say that Nelle has written another book, called *The Reverend*, but it is in an undisclosed vault and to be published posthumously. The book, if it exists, is said to be the story of a true crime, written in the vein of *In Cold Blood*. The subject is a deceased minister, Reverend William Maxwell, from eastern Alabama, who was a practitioner of voodoo. Maxwell was most notorious for the fact that five of his relatives died under mysterious circumstances, and he was the beneficiary of each victim's life insurance policy. At the fifth funeral service another relative got even and killed Maxwell.

Nelle lived in Alex City, Alabama, for a time in the 1980s to research the case. Maxwell's lawyer, Tom Radney, who gave her the case files to study, said, "I found Nelle Lee to be warm, charming, and extremely intelligent. She is not a recluse by any means. I think the reason she doesn't like publicity is, to her, that would be flaunting her success. And she's not that type." Nelle was also given files of background information by journalist Jim Earnhardt, who covered the trials. Wayne Greenhaw said she quit writing the book because it was going to wind up being more about the insurance companies than the crime itself, but others say the book exists. In 1997 Radney said, "I still talk to Nelle twice a year, and every time we talk she says she's still working on it."

Nelle once told a friend, "I gave up my life for one book and the lives of my family members. Why would I do it for another?"

It is hoped that she has written *The Reverend*. But it will not be published during her lifetime.

Source Notes

FOREWORD

"Hell no! . . .": Childress, "Looking for Harper Lee."

"I may be . . .": Letter from Nelle Harper Lee to author.

"Real courage is . . .": Lee, *To Kill a Mockingbird*, 121.

"a beautiful, remarkable . . .": Greenhaw, *Alabama on My Mind*, 100.

hates eggs . . .: Williams, "Little Nelle Heads Ram, Maps Lee's Strategy."

Russian Tea Room . . .: Greenhaw, author interview.

"Miss Lee and I . . .": Greenhaw, *Ghosts on the Road*, 14.
"She was so . . .": Hines, author interview.

INTRODUCTION

"comes from a . . .": Kemp, "Mockingbird Won't Sing."

"I'm afraid . . ." and "play" and "reading, golf, and . . . ": Lee, letter to Huntingdon College.

OVERVIEW

It must have . . .: Bell, author interview.

"haint . . .": Lee, *To Kill a Mockingbird*, 19.

"Anybody who has . . .": Holmes, "Queen of the Birds."

"clime and tone . . ." and "argue cases . . .": Hutchens, "It Is and It Isn't Autobiographical."

"*Mockingbird*" and "preamble": Lee, Foreword to 35th anniversary edition of *To Kill a Mockingbird*, 1.

CHAPTER ONE

"queen of the . . .": Jones, *Happenings in Old Monroeville*, 125.

"Like a freight . . .": Rosborough, author interview.

"Dody," "Bear," "Weezie," "Brother": Shields, *Mockingbird*, 41.

"nervous disorder . . .": Mills, "A Life Apart."

"Mrs. Busybody . . .": Grobel, *Conversations with Capote*, 53.

"Get out of . . .": Jones, author interview.

"You're certainly a . . .": Blass, author interview.

But in a letter…: *O Magazine*, "A Letter from Harper Lee."

"Truman's vicious lie . . .": Shields, *Mockingbird*, 270.

"We in America . . .": Nash, *American Odyssey*, 332.

"experienced by the . . .": Nash, *American Odyssey*, 324.

"Let me assert . . .": Nash, *American Odyssey*, 360.

"life was grim . . .": Deitch, "Harper Lee."

"She was raised": Giddens-White, *The Story Behind*, 28.

"their lives were . . .": Moates, Truman Capote's Southern Years, 35.

"When we were. . .": Greenhaw, *Alabama on My Mind*, 104.

"Ed was real . . .": Skinner, author interview.

"If I went . . .": Newquist, *Counterpoint*, 407.

"When we were children . . .": Plimpton, *Truman Capote*, 15.

mother, an alcoholic. . . .: Carter, author interview.

"We did not . . .": Newquist, *Counterpoint*, 407.

"He must have . . .": Greenhaw, *Alabama on My Mind*, 103.

CHAPTER TWO

A mustard poultice: Butts, author interview.

"the store . . .": Monroe County Heritage Museums, Monroeville, 60.

"that sparkled with . . .": Park, "Truman's Aunt Tiny."

"Books were scarce . . .": Lee, Harper, Letter to *O*.

Several black women . . .: Jones, author interview.

"one-graining it . . .": Jones, author interview.

Rubber-band guns, Nelle's love for Aunt Sook . . .: Carter, author interview.

smelly feet of customers . . .: Clarke, *Capote, A Biography*, 15.

"the grass harp . . .": Capote, *The Grass Harp.*

Monroe County Elementary . . .: Farish, author interview.

"impatient" and "ignored": Lee, Letter to O.

"extremely bored by . . .": Associated Press, "Luckiest Person in World."

"I went home . . .": Farish, author interview.

James A. York . . .: Jones, author interview.

"Hot Grease in the kitchen . . .": Jones, author interview.

"She was tough on me . . .": Shields, *Mockingbird*, 47.

"Sissy . . .": Clarke, *Capote*, 42.

"I didn't feel . . .": Clarke, *Capote*, 43.

"Pedal, Big Boy . . .": Moates, *Truman Capote's Southern Years*, 103.

Ninety-degree angle . . .: Clark, author interview.

A crop-duster . . .: Jones, author interview.

Her salary was . . .: Tucker, author interview.

"one that will . . .": Moates, *Truman Capote's Southern Years*, 51.

John White . . .: Moates, *Truman Capote's Southern Years*, 53.

"a tragedy" and rarely ever left . . .: Skinner, author interview.

pale white hand . . .: Blass, author interview.

"One-hundred percent . . .": Kyvig, *Daily Life*, 142.

"I wasn't going . . ." and "See what your . . .": Moates, *Truman Capote's Southern Years*, 62.

"In my original version . . .": Nance, *The Worlds of Truman Capote*, 223.

"To live in . . .": Shields, *Mockingbird*, 54.

CHAPTER THREE

"Yellow Mama . . .": Battilana, author interview.

The National Association . . .: Horne, *Powell v. Alabama*, 30–31.

"The economic collapse . . .": Johnson, *Understanding* To Kill a Mockingbird, 16.

"a Jew lawyer from . . .": "Scottsboro: An American Tragedy."

"There are heroes . . .": "Scottsboro: An American Tragedy."

"Walter Lett, alias. . .": *Monroe Journal*. "Negro Held for Attacking Woman."

"leading citizen": *Monroe Journal*. "Lett Negro Saved from Electric Chair."

some scholars decided. . .: Clark, author interview.

In the late . . .: Mallon, "Big Bird."

"Two Negroes Executed. . .": *Monroe Journal*, "Two Negroes Executed."

"The year of . . .": Stallworth, "Miss Alice Lee's Life in Law."

CHAPTER FOUR

"I thought we . . ." "Can I play . . ." "Sure is hot . . ." and "We either ordered . . .": Blass, author interview.

"clarity, coherence, cadence . . .": Shields, *Mockingbird*, 64.

Monroe County High . . .: Jones, author interview.

"There's no substitute . . .": Newquist, *Counterpoint*, 409.

Queenie, Sook's dog . . .: Carter, author interview.

After Alice left . . .: Butts, Bar Association Speech.

"The Victory Tax . . ." and "Atticus in a skirt . . .": Butts, Bar Association Speech.

Nelle preferred brushing . . .: Shields, Mockingbird, 76.

"She wasn't worried . . .": Shields, Mockingbird, 77.

"Those conversations were . . .": Shields, Mockingbird, 75.

CHAPTER FIVE

"specialized in blondes . . .": Shields, *Mockingbird*, 84.

"Finally someone hit . . .": Shields, *Mockingbird*, 86–87.

"second home . . .": Kipen, "The Big Read: Harper Lee's *To Kill a Mockingbird*, 4.

"In case you've . . ." and "An impressive figure . . .": Williams, "Little Nelle Heads Ram."

"I don't know . . .": Shields, *Mockingbird*, 98.

"he claimed her . . .": Greenhaw, author interview.

"Miss Nelle Lee . . .": Nettles, "Miss Nelle Lee Chosen to Attend Oxford."

"A short novel . . .": Clarke, *Capote*, 156.

And it was exactly. . .: Clark, author interview.

"the itch": Mills, "A Life Apart."

CHAPTER SIX

He was in a position . . .: Flynt, author interview.

"Miss Lee Accepts . . .": Nettles, "Miss Lee Accepts Position in New York."

"All the Southerners . . .": Shields, *Mockingbird*, 22.

"Until I came . . ." Mitchell, *My Ears Are Bent*, 5.

Metropolitan Museum of Art . . .: Butts, author interview.

"Nelle Lee is no . . .": Waller, "To Kill a Mockingbird."

A little out of shape . . .: Skinner, author interview.

"I walked around . . .": Hellmuth, "Walking in Harper Lee's Shoes."

"I missed Christmas . . ." and "We haven't forgotten . . .": Lee, "What Christmas Means to Me," 63.

"The one string . . .": *Alabama Alumni News*, "Alumna Wins Pulitzer . . ."

"On a hot . . ." "It was real . . ." and "more of series . . .": Hohoff, "We Get a New Author," 3–4.

"an advance of . . .": Shields, *I Am Scout*, 90.

"teeth were made . . ." and "a vivid and . . .": Hohoff, "We Get a New Author," 3–4.

"like building a . . .": Deitch, "Harper Lee."

"There were dangling. . .": Hohoff, "We Get a New Author," 3–4.

"Yes, it is . . .": Mitchell, "Unseen Capote."

"On July 11 . . .": Clarke, *Too Brief a Treat*, 284.

CHAPTER SEVEN

"It was deep . . .": "In Cold Blood."

"WEALTHY FARMER, 3 . . .": Clarke, *Capote, A Biography*, 317.

"merciful.": Newquist, *Counterpoint*, 405.

"Waldorf of the Praries . . .": Shields, *Mockingbird*, 136.

"Foxy . . .": Clarke, *Capote*, 324.

"No access.": Clarke, *Capote*, 321.

"He was afraid . . .": Clarke, *Capote*, 319.

"It looked as . . .": "In Cold Blood."

"an absolutely fantastic . . .": Plimpton, *Truman Capote*, 170.

"Nelle walked into . . .": Clarke, *Capote*, 322.

"I cannot get . . ." and "Hang on. You . . .": Clarke, *Capote*, 323.

"She is a . . .": Plimpton, *Truman Capote*, 199.

"Cast herself in . . .": *Montgomery Advertiser*, "World-Famous Authors Were Childhood Pals."

"fact-finding" and "mood gathering . . .": *Montgomery Advertiser*, "World-Famous Authors Were Childhood Pals."

"I had this . . ." and "I thought it . . .": "In Cold Blood."

"For Capote, the . . .": Klein, "Film 'Capote' Raises Disturbing Ethical Questions."

CHAPTER EIGHT

"Someone rare has. . .": Shields, *Mockingbird*, 14.

"The dialogue of . . .": Lyell, F. H. Review of *To Kill a Mockingbird*.

"Miss Lee is . . .": *The New Yorker*, Review of *To Kill a Mockingbird*.

"The novel is . . .": McMichael, Review of *To Kill a Mockingbird*.

"So admirably done . . .": Sullivan, Review of *To Kill a Mockingbird*.

"melodramatic . . .": *Booklist*, Review of *To Kill a Mockingbird*.

"frankly and completely . . .": Adams, Review of *To Kill a Mockingbird*.

"Harper Lee has . . ." and "The old legends . . .": Hohoff, "We Get a New Author," 3–4

"Impressive information, but": Nettles, "New Claim to Literary Fame."

"In this day . . .": and "Dear Sir or. . ." *Newsweek*.

"My book has . . ." and "It amuses me . . .": Allison, "'Mockingbird' Author is Alabama's"   "Although publishers have . . .": Nettles, "New Claim to Literary Fame."

"I never dreamed . . .": Hendrix, "Monroeville Attorney's Reactions Varied."

"It was also . . .": Hutchens, "It Is and It Isn't."

"Had a note . . .": Clarke, *Too Brief a Treat*, 299.

"I talked with. . .": "State Pulitzer Winner Too Busy to Write."

"The Long Goodbye . . ." Shields, *Mockingbird*, 115.

"I've found I . . .": Lawrence, "Author's Problem."

"I am more . . .": Boyle, "Harper Lee Running."

"luckiest woman in . . .": "'Luckiest Person in the World' says Pulitzer Winner."

 "it told the . . ." and "I never wanted . . .": Welch, *Mockingbird Summers*.

"*To Kill a* . . .": McCoy, *Monroeville*, 81.

"This book is . . .": "Chicago Press Call."

"How did the . . ." "Southern lawyers don't . . ." "That's a large . . ." "the name Harper . . ." "Yes. Recently, I . . .": and "With reluctance . . .": "Chicago Press Call."

"I cling to . . .": Deitch, "Harper Lee."

"We had a . . .": Farish, author interview.

CHAPTER NINE

There was no . . .: Kowars, *The Kacey Kowars Radio Show*.

"an actor's director . . .": Kiselyak, *Fearful Symmetry,* Horton Foote speaking.

"From the very . . .": Shields, *Mockingbird,* 195.

"The sale is . . .": Shields, *Mockingbird,* 193.

"I was close . . .": and "I don't want . . .": Kowars, *The Kacey Kowars Radio Show.*

"I couldn't find . . ." and "The minute that . . .": Kiselyak, *Fearful Symmetry,* Horton Foote speaking.

"Dear Alan, I . . .": Bumstead, Letter to Alan Pakula.

"If you want . . .": Kiselyak, *Fearful Symmetry,* Gregory Peck speaking.

Now, that was . . .: Farish, author interview.

"We checked the . . .": Moorer, author interview.

"I know authors. . .": Thomas, "Harper Lee Returns Visits."

In fact, every . . .: Kiselyak, *Fearful Symmetry.*

"Wonderful. First take. . . ." "pretty puffed up" "Harper, did I . . ." and "Oh Gregory, you've . . . great acting.": Kiselyak, *Fearful Symmetry,* Gregory Peck speaking.

"My father is . . .": Keith, "An Afternoon with Harper Lee."

"Lee, a great . . .": Hendrix, "Firm Gives Books to Monroe County."

"I have tried . . .": Hendrix, "Monroeville Impresses Visiting Movie Star."

"Given in memory . . .": Hendrix, "Firm Gives Books to Monroe County."

"Universal hated the . . .": Kowars, *The Kasey Kowars Radio Show,* Horton Foote speaking.

"Beware of your . . .": Mulligan, *To Kill a Mockingbird.*

"I understand that . . .": "Chicago Press Call."

"It does not . . .": Nettles, "Pulitzer Prize-Winner Harper Lee Entertains."

"I had a . . .": Thomas, "Clutching Miss Lee's Dad's Watch."

"Dear Editor . . .": Lee, Letter to the Editor.

"They treated it . . .": "Keith, "An Afternoon with Harper Lee."

"It tore my . . .": Mulligan, *To Kill a Mockingbird*.

"Dearhearts . . .": Clarke, *Too Brief a Treat*, 382.

CHAPTER TEN

"Well, the first . . .": Newquist, *Counterpoint*, 410.

"It was like . . .": Newquist, *Counterpoint*, 405.

"Nelle would call . . .": Jones, author interview.

"Nelle is in . . .": Clarke, *Too Brief a Treat*, 412.

"If more young . . .": Lee, "When Children Discover America."

"Nelle just went . . .": Romine, "Two writers."

Nelle had adored . . .: Greenhaw, author interview.

"Her letters are . . .": Mills, "A Life Apart."

"It's like an owl . . .": Anonymous, author interview.

"As far as . . .": Clarke, e-mail to author.

"He never won . . ." and "Truman's ego would . . .": Flynt, author interview.

"I don't like . . .": Hogan, "George Plimpton."

"I'm always a . . .": Garbarino, "Greetings from Monroeville."

"They always see . . .": Bellafante, "Harper Lee, Gregarious for a Day."

"Oh my God . . .": Wolfson, "Majority Black, White."

"The idea of . . .": Jaffe, author interview.

"revitalize . . .": Gioia, Preface to "The Big Read," 1.

"We had a . . .": Revoyr, author interview.

"After reading the . . .": Womble, author interview.

"I met Nelle . . .": Roberts, author interview.

A family with . . .and "Dear Nelle, I . . .": Jones, author interview.

"It's better to . . .": Associated Press August 20, 2007, "Harper Lee Briefly."

"At a critical . . .": White House, Office of the Press Secretary, "President Bush Announces."

"It's 1935 and . . ." McCorvey, *Playbill*.

"Now 75 years . . .": Buncombe, "Oprah Winfrey."

"the first one . . .": Greenhaw, author interview.

"New York is . . .": Butts, author interview.

"We go out . . .": Mills, "A Life Apart."

"I wish she . . .": Kemp, "The Elusive—But Still Alive—Harper Lee."

"has become the . . .": Associated Press, "Harper Lee, Attorney At Law."

"You know, many . . .": Newquist, *Counterpoint*, 405.

"I asked her once . . .": Monroe County Heritage Museums, *Monroeville*, 86.

Reliable sources . . .: Anonymous, author interview.

"I found Nelle. . ." and "I still talk . . .": Kemp, "The Elusive—But Still Alive—Harper Lee."

Nelle once told . . .: Anonymous, author interview.

Bibliography

Adams, Phoebe. Review of *To Kill a Mockingbird*. *Atlantic*, August 1960.

Alabama Alumni News. "Alumna Wins Pulitzer Prize for Distinguished Fiction." May–June, 1961.

Allison, Ramona. "'Mockingbird' Author is Alabama's 'Woman of Year,'" *Birmingham Post Herald*, January 3, 1962.

Arnett, Matt. Author interview, e-mail and phone, 2008.

Associated Press. "Harper Lee, Attorney At Law." May 16, 2008.

———. "Harper Lee Becomes Special Member of Alabama State Bar." May 16, 2008.

———. "Harper Lee Briefly Breaks Usual Public Silence at Alabama Academy of Honor Ceremony." August 20, 2007.

———. "'Luckiest Person in World' says Pulitzer Prize winner." May 2, 1961.

———. "Parents Claim Racism in Harper Lee's Alabama Hometown." May 24, 2008.

Battilana, Martin. Author interview. Monroeville, Alabama, 2007.

Bell, Helen Norris. Author interview. Black Mountain, North Carolina, 2007.

Bellafante, Ginia. "Harper Lee, Gregarious for a Day." *The New York Times*, January 30, 2006.

Benn, Alvin. *Reporter: Covering Civil Rights . . . and Wrongs in Dixie*. Bloomington, Indiana: Author House, 2006.

Blass, A. B. Author interviews. Monroeville, Alabama, 2007, 2008.

Booklist. Review of *To Kill a Mockingbird*. July 1960.

Boyle, Hal. "Harper Lee Running Scared Getting Fat on Heels of Success." *Birmingham News*, March 15, 1963.

Brown, Hanna. Author interviews. Monroeville, Alabama, 2007, 2008.

Brown, Mary Ward. Author interviews. Marion, Alabama, 2007, 2008.

Brown, Susan. Author interviews. Monroeville, Alabama, 2007, 2008.

Bumstead, Henry. Letter to Alan Pakula Archives at Monroe County Heritage Museums, November 1961.

Buncombe, Andrew. "Oprah Winfrey Persuades Harper Lee to Write after Years of Silence." *Independent*, June 28, 2006.

Butts, Reverend Thomas Lane. Author interview. Monroeville, Alabama, 2007, 2008.

———. Bar Association speech. "An Introduction of Alice Finch Lee as Recipient of the 2003 Maud McClure Kelly Award by the Alabama Bar Association," July 18, 2003.

Cannon, Vivian. "Mockingbird Author Wants to Disappear." *Mobile Register*, March 21, 1963.

Capote, Truman. *The Complete Stories of Truman Capote*. New York: Vintage International, A Division of Random House, 2004.

———. *In Cold Blood*. New York: Vintage International, A Division of Random House, 1965, 1994.

———. *Other Rooms, Other Voices*. New York: Vintage International, A Division of Random House, 1948, 1975.

Carter, Jennings "Big Boy." Author interview. Monroeville, Alabama, 2007.

"Chicago Press Call," *Rogue*. December 1963, vol. 9, no. 12.

Childress, Mark. "Looking for Harper Lee." *Southern Living*, May 1997, 148–150.

Clark, Jane Ellen. Author interview. Monroeville, Alabama, 2007, 2008.

Clarke, Gerald. Author interview, e-mail, 2007.

———. *Capote: A Biography*. New York: Carroll & Graf Publishers, 1988.

———. *too brief a treat: The Letters of Truman Capote*, Random House, 2004.

Deitch, Joseph. "Harper Lee: Novelist of the South: Conscientious Writer." *Christian Science Monitor*, October 3, 1961.

Farish, Anne. Author interview. Monroeville, Alabama, 2007.

Flynt, Dr. Wayne. Author interview, e-mail and phone, 2007.

Garbarino, Steve. "Greetings from Monroeville." *Blackbook*, July 30, 2007, 66–73.

Giddens-White, Bryon. *The Story Behind . . . Harper Lee's* To Kill a Mockingbird. Chicago, Illinois: Heinemann Library, 2007.

Gioia, Dana. Preface to "The Big Read: Harper Lee's *To Kill a Mockingbird*." National Endowment for the Arts "The Big Read" program, 2006, 1.

Grammer, Dr. John. Author interview. Sewanee, Tennessee, 2007.

Greenhaw, Wayne. *Alabama on My Mind*. Alabama: Sycamore Press, 1987.

———. Author interview. Montgomery, Alabama, 2007.

———. *Ghosts on the Road Poems of Alabama, Mexico and Beyond*. Montgomery, Alabama: River City Publishing, 2007.

Grobel, Lawrence. *Conversations with Capote*. Cambridge, Massachusetts: Da Capo Press, 1985.

Hellmuth, Ann. "Walking in Harper Lee's Shoes," *Orlando Sentinel*, June 11, 2006.

Hendrix, Vernon. "Monroeville Attorney's Reactions Varied over Daughter's Book." *Monroe Journal*, September 8, 1960.

———. "Monroeville Impresses Visiting Movie Star." *Montgomery Advertiser*, January 6, 1962.

———. "Firm Gives Books to Monroe County." *Montgomery Advertiser*, December 23, 1962.

———. "World-Famous Authors were Childhood Pals." *Montgomery Advertiser*, October 11, 1964.

Hines, Jacqueline "Bunny." Author interview. Monroeville, Alabama, 2007.

Hogan, Ron. "George Plimpton," *Beatrice: The Collected Interviews, 1997.* http://www.beatrice.com/interviews/plimpton/

Hohoff, Tay. "We Get a New Author." *Literary Guild Book Club Magazine*, August 1960, 3–4.

Holmes, Molly. "Queen of the Birds." *The South* magazine, April/May 2008. http://www.thesouthmag.com/readArticle.asp ?deptID=29&id=447

Horne, Gerald. *Powell v. Alabama: The Scottsboro Boys and American Justice.* Danbury Connecticut: Franklin Watts, Grolier Publishing, 1997.

Hutchens, John K. "It Is and It Isn't Autobiographical." *New York Herald Tribune*, 1962.

"In Cold Blood…An American Tragedy." *Newsweek*, January 24, 1966, 59–61.

Jaffe, Sandy. Author interview, e-mail and phone, 2008.

Johnson, Claudia Durst. *Understanding* To Kill a Mockingbird: *A Student Casebook to Issues, Sources, and Historic Documents.* Westport, Connecticut: Greenwood Press, Literature in Context Series, 1994.

Jones, George Thomas. Author interview. Monroeville, Alabama, 2007, 2008.

———. *Happenings in Old Monroeville, Volume 1*. Monroeville, Alabama: Bolton Newspapers, 1999.

———. *Happenings in Old Monroeville, Volume 2*. Monroeville, Alabama: Bolton Newspapers, 2003.

Keith, Don Lee. "An Afternoon with Harper Lee." *Delta Review*, Spring 1966, 40–41, 75, 80–81.

Kemp, Kathy. "The Elusive—But Still Alive—Harper Lee." *Scripps Howard News Service*, November 2, 1997.

Kipen, David, and Erika Koss. "The Big Read: Harper Lee's *To Kill a Mockingbird*." National Endowment for the Arts "The Big Read" program, 2006, 2–13.

Kiselyak, Charles. (Writer/Director/Producer), *Fearful Symmetry: The Making of To Kill a Mockingbird*, Universal Home Video, 1998.

Klein, Peter. "Film 'Capote' Raises Disturbing Ethical Questions." *Journalism Ethics*, January 2006. http://www.journalismethics.ca/book_reviews/capote.htm

Kowars, Kacey. *The Kacey Kowars Radio Show*, December 6, 2004. http://www.kaceykowarsshow.com/authors/foote.html

Kyvig, David E. *Daily Life in The United States, 1920-1939, Decades of Promise and Pain*. Westport Connecticut: Greenwood Press, 2002.

Lawrence, Wes. "Author's Problem: Friends." *Cleveland Plain Dealer*, March 17, 1964.

Lee, A. C. (editor). "Death Sentence Given to Negro." *Monroe*

Journal, March 29, 1934.

———."Lett Negro Given Reprieve by Governor." *Monroe Journal*, May 17, 1934.

———."Lett Negro Saved from Electric Chair." *Monroe Journal*, July 12, 1934.

———."Monroe County Negro Gets Second Reprieve." *Monroe Journal*, June 21, 1934.

———." Negro Held for Attacking Woman." *Monroe Journal*, November 3, 1933.

Lee, Harper. "Caustic Comment." *Crimson White*, June 28, 1946.

———. "Christmas to Me." *McCall's*, December 1961, 63.

———. Foreword to the 35th anniversary edition of *To Kill a Mockingbird*. New York: HarperCollins, 1993.

———. Letter to Huntingdon College, Houghton Memorial Library, January 26, 1961.

———. Letter to O, July 2006.

———. Letter to the editor: *Monroe Journal*, February 1963.

———. "Romance and High Adventure." *Clearings in the Thicket*, Mercer College, 1985.

———. *To Kill a Mockingbird*. New York: J. B. Lippincott, 1960.

———. "When Children Discover America." *McCall's*, August 1965.

"'Luckiest Person in the World' says Pulitzer Winner." *Publishers Weekly*, May 2, 1961

Lyell, F. H. Review of *To Kill a Mockingbird. New York Times Book Review*, July 10, 1960, 5.

Mallon, Thomas. "Big Bird: A Biography of the Novelist Harper Lee." *New Yorker*, May 29, 2006, 79–81.

McCorvey, Charlie. "To Kill a Mockingbird," *Playbill*. Monroeville, 2008.

McCoy, Kathy. *Monroeville: Literary Capital of Alabama*. Charleston, South Carolina: Arcadia Publishing, 1998.

McMichael, George. Review of *To Kill a Mockingbird. San Francisco Chronicle*, July 21, 1960.

Mills, Marja. "A Life Apart: Harper Lee, The Complex Woman Behind 'A Delicious Mystery.'" *Chicago Tribune*, September 13, 2002.

Mitchell, Garry. "Unseen Capote." *The Decatur Daily*, April 23, 2006.

Mitchell, Joseph. *My Ears Are Bent*. Vintage, (reprint.) 2008.

Moates, Marianne. *Truman Capote's Southern Years: Stories from a Monroeville Cousin*. The University of Alabama Press, 1989.

"Mocking Bird Call." *Newsweek*, January 4, 1961, 83.

Monroe County Heritage Museums. *Monroeville: The Search for Harper Lee's Maycomb*. Charleston, South Carolina: Arcadia Publishing, 1999.

Moorer, Martha Louise Jones. Author interview. Monroeville,

Alabama, 2007.

Mulligan, Robert. *To Kill a Mockingbird,* feature commentary. Two-Disc Special Edition DVD, Universal Home Video, 2005.

Nance, William. *The Worlds of Truman Capote.* New York: Stein and Day, 1970.

Nash, Gary B. *American Odyssey: The United States in the Twentieth Century.* New York: McGraw-Hill, 1996.

Nettles, Frances. "Miss Lee Accepts Position in New York." *Monroe Journal,* 1949.

————. "Miss Nelle Lee Chosen to Attend Oxford." *Monroe Journal,* April 7, 1948.

————. "New Claim to Literary Fame." *Monroe Journal,* June 2, 1960.

————. "Pulitzer Prize-Winner Harper Lee Entertains Star Gregory Peck Here." *Monroe Journal,* January 18, 1962.

The New Yorker. Review of *To Kill a Mockingbird.* July 1960.

Newman, Cathy. "To Catch a Mockingbird." *National Geographic,* January 2006, 114-22.

Newquist, Roy. *Counterpoint.* Chicago: Rand McNally, 1964.

Park, Mary Jane. "Truman's Aunt Tiny." *St. Petersburg Times,* October 3, 2000.

Pickett, Albert James. *Pickett's History of Alabama.* River City, Alabama: River City Publishing, 1851.

Plimpton, George. *Truman Capote: In Which Various Friends,*

Enemies, Acquaintances, and Detractors Recall His Turbulent Career. New York: Doubleday, 1998.

Revoyr, Nina. Author interview. Los Angeles, California, 2008.

Roberts, Angela. Author interview. Monroeville, Alabama 2007.

Robertson, Nan. "Johnson Hails the Creative Life with a Dinner at White House." *New York Times*, December 14, 1966.

Romine, Dannye. "Two Writers . . . and a Small Alabama Town." *Birmingham News*, September 30, 1977.

Rosborough, Jane Hybart. Author interview. Tuscaloosa, Alabama, 2007.

Rowley, Hazel. "Mockingbird Country." *Australian Review of Books*, April 1999. http://www.hazelrowley.com/mockingbird. html

Rudisill, Marie. *The Southern Haunting of Truman Capote.* Nashville, Tennessee: Cumberland House, 2000.

Scenes and Stories of Monroeville: "To Kill a Mockingbird" Teacher Workshop. DVD. Monroe County Heritage Museums, 2007.

"Scottsboro: An American Tragedy." PBS American Experience. http://www.pbs.org/wgbh/amex/scottsboro/peopleevents/p_ild. html.

Shields, Charles. *I Am Scout: The Biography of Harper Lee.* New York: Henry Holt and Company, 2008.

———. *Mockingbird: A Portrait of Harper Lee.* New York: Henry Holt and Company, 2006.

Skinner, Charles Ray. Author interview. Monroeville, Alabama, 2007.

Stallworth, Clarke. "Miss Alice Lee's Life in Law Has Given Her Satisfaction Akin to Her Noted Sister's." *Birmingham News*, February, 1982.

"State Pulitzer Prize Winner Too Busy to Write." *Dothan Eagle*, May 2, 1961.

Sullivan, Richard. "Review of *To Kill a Mockingbird*." *Chicago Tribune*, July 17, 1960.

Thomas, Bob. "Clutching Miss Lee's Dad's Watch, Peck Wins Oscar." The Associated Press, April 9, 1963.

————. "Harper Lee Returns Visits: Sees Movies Sets, Hollywood." *Monroe Journal*, February 9, 1962.

Thompson, Katherine. Author interview, e-mail, 2007.

Tucker, Mary. Author interview, conducted with George Thomas Jones, 2008.

"Two Negroes Executed." *Monroe Journal*, December 25, 1919.

Waller, Ruth. "To Kill a Mockingbird." *Montgomery Advertiser*, July 14, 1960.

Welch, Dale. *Mockingbird Summers: Visits with the Citizens of Monroeville*. DVD Documentary. Monroe County Heritage Museums, 2006.

White House, Office of the Press Secretary. "President Bush Announces Recipients of Presidential Medal of Freedom." October 29, 2007. http://www.whitehouse.gov/news/releases/2007/10/20071029.html

Williams, Mary. "Little Nelle Heads Ram, Maps Lee's Strategy." *Crimson White*, October 8, 1946.

Windham, Donald. *Lost Friendships: A Memoir of Truman Capote, Tennessee Williams, and Others*. New York: William Morrow, 1983.

Windham, Kathryn Tucker. Author interview. Selma, Alabama, 2007.

———. *Ernest's Gift*. Montgomery, Alabama: Junebug Books, 2004.

———. *Odd Egg Editor*. Jackson, Mississippi: University of Mississippi Press, 1990.

Wolfson, Hannah. "Majority Black, White Schools Unite to Stage *To Kill a Mockingbird*," *Birmingham News*, September 14, 2006.

Womble, Nancy. Author interview. Monroeville, Alabama 2007.

Index

Note: Page numbers in *italics* indicate photos

Acknowledgments

I AM MOST grateful to my editor, Catherine Frank, who asked me to write this book. Three trips to Alabama later and over a year's worth of research along with intense rewrites and revisions, I feel a fondness and bond with all the stories and people I never would have known. Catherine is like Tay Hohoff, Harper Lee's beloved editor. She knew which questions to ask and how to help me shape the material into a story. Because of her, I had the remarkable opportunity to interview people who are in their eighties and even nineties, and the stories they told of their own lives could fill many more books than this one biography. Also in the Viking Children's Books family, I so appreciate the support of Regina Hayes, Kendra Levin, Derry Wilkens, and Jim Hoover's jacket design and Janet Pascal's copy edits.

I would like to thank the staff at the Monroe County Heritage Museum, especially Jane Ellen Clark, who is a font of knowledge of Alabama history. Staff members Stephanie Rogers and Monica Helton located elusive dates and names on articles, and Dora Bullard and Barbara Wilson were so helpful to me during my visits to the Courthouse, and Cole Champion always sent me requested materials. The staff took the time to answer questions and give me guidance and insight into Nelle Harper Lee's world of Monroeville, Alabama.

I am deeply indebted to Professor John Grammer at the University of the South in Sewanee who first wrote a letter of introduction to Miss Lee on my behalf, and I am also so thankful to Loretta Ellsworth, author of *In Search of Mockingbird*, who sent me many materials and books from the very start of my research.

Visiting with Truman Capote's cousin, Jennings Carter, was like stepping back in time, listening to his stories of wild plum pie, shelling peas, and going to the swimming hole. His gentle kindness as a storyteller painted a picture of an Alabama childhood filled with adventures. His most memorable lines were "Truman just liked to put on. He was as strong as anybody and could walk on his hands all the way down the road." He smiled and said, "As for Nelle, we didn't even know she was a girl."

I would like to thank Jay Lamar and Elizabeth Panhorst at the Alabama Center for the Book, who put me in touch with so many wonderful Alabama folks. I will forever treasure my talks with Wayne Greenhaw, Angela Roberts, and Reverend Thomas Lane Butts and his beautiful wife, Hilda, who is a spirit of love and generosity. I am incredibly thankful to the Monroe County Librarian, Jacqueline "Bunny" Hines, and her assistant, Louise Brown, who aided me with research and showed me around the library, the former site of the hotel where Gregory Peck stayed in 1962. Bunny's sister, Anne Hines, the former mayor of Monroeville and a classmate of Nelle Harper Lee's, also gave detailed descriptions of school and rituals of growing up in Monroeville. Jane Hybart Rosborough welcomed me into her home and told me stories of her childhood and dressing up like a sack of fertilizer for the parade in the town square and admitted, "I didn't like it one bit."

Martin Battilana was a great help with his luminous pictures of the Mockingbird Players, and he also showed me and my sister, Keely, how to cross the Alabama River on a three-car ferry that runs on an old school bus engine. That adventure eventually led me to Monroe Intermediate School in Lower Peachtree for a wonderful author visit with seventy-five students in this K-8 country school through Alabama Voices.

Aaron White of Monroeville, Alabama, provided invaluable old photographs from the Max McAliley Collection. Mary Tucker's stories on the documentary *Mockingbird Summers* and columns by her daughter, Cynthia Tucker also provided me with a greater knowledge and understanding of Monroeville, Alabama.

I am thankful to A. B. Blass, who took us on a tour of Monroeville and gave so generously of his time and stories. As a boy, he once climbed into the old clock tower of the Courthouse to hit the bell with the iron clock winder to make the clock strike thirteen. The next day folks at church whispered, "Did you hear the clock struck thirteen times last night?" He also defied the KKK when they announced that the black high school would not be allowed to march in the annual Monroeville Christmas Parade in 1959. Instead of giving in to their threats and demands, A. B. canceled the parade and faced the wrath of the Klan, but Mr. A. C. Lee told him, "You did the right thing, son. You did right."

George Thomas Jones could rival any New York researcher with the speed at which he could respond to questions from topics as diverse as hoop cheese to fires in Monroeville to attending a George Washington Carver lecture in 1934 at the Courthouse. From Hoover carts to Mr. A. C. Lee's jerky golf swing to a smart al-eck Truman Capote ordering a "Broadway Flip" when George was working as a soda jerk on the Square, he had a story for everything. George also arranged for me to meet with Charles Ray Skinner, a childhood friend and football teammate of the late Ed Lee, Nelle Harper Lee's brother, and his detailed recollections of Monroe-ville proved invaluable to me.

I would also like to thank Hanna Brown and her beautiful mother, Alma Susan Brown, who opened their home to me and to my daughter, Norah, and gave us di-rections on the back roads and descriptions of contem-porary life in Monroeville. Hanna has played Scout and Mayella for the Mockingbird Players and figures she may graduate one day to be Miss Stephanie or Miss Maudie.

I met Dr. Nancy Anderson in 1996 when my first novel was published, and I have the deepest admiration and respect for her. Nancy invited me to work with at-risk children in Montgomery, Alabama, at the Mo-lina Center, with my own daughter, Norah, who loved her first trip to Alabama. Harper Lee's silence led me also to three authors of her generation: Kathryn Tucker Windham, Mary Ward Brown, and Helen Norris Bell, and Nancy helped me get interviews with all three authors, and although I had originally intended to talk to them about Harper Lee, their own stories filled a thirty-page essay on the writing life published in *Five Points: A Journal of Art and Literature*. My agent and friend, Marianne Merola, knew that the stories of these amazing Alabama women (with three hundred years of storytelling between them) had to find a home, and she found one at *Five Points*. I feel so lucky for Marianne's wisdom and humor with her straight-to-the-point observations.

I would like to thank Cheryl and Thomas Upchurch of Capitol Books, whose stories have made every trip to Alabama that much more interesting and lively. Claudia Durst Johnson was a guide for me both in her book and in her words in *Fearful Symmetry*, a documentary about the making of *To Kill a Mockingbird*. Lillian Johnson was also so helpful in her quick responses and questions, making sure I had the quotes correct.

I am incredibly grateful to Dr. Wayne Flynt, who took the time to talk to me and whose essays of Alabama history have been a tremendous resource. Dr. Flynt also said that Charles Shields's unofficial biography, *Mockingbird*, was most beneficial in proving how much Harper Lee helped Truman Capote in his research in Kansas, and his book was a great help to me in my research, as was Marianne Moates's book *Truman Capote's Southern Years*.

Mary Ann Pickard from Huntingdon College and Jessica Lacher-Feldman from the University of Alabama were most helpful in providing pictures and stories of Nelle Harper Lee's days as a university student.

I am very grateful to Vicki Palmquist of the Children's Literature Network, who advised me to talk to Loretta Ellsworth, author of *In Search of Mockingbird*. Loretta sent me books and articles, and told me stories of her recent trip to Monroeville with her own sister and meeting the late Dickie Williams, who owned a store on the town square and shared his stories with her.

Matt Arnett's descriptions of Gee's Bend and his assistance in finding me the date that Martin Luther King traveled to Gee's Bend, Alabama, was a gift. So was meeting biographer Elizabeth Partridge at the Georgia O'Keefe Ghost Ranch as part of Kindling Words West. Her candor and careful review of my early chapters helped me clarify and rethink how to approach this biography, and I am most indebted to her kindness and honesty. I would also like to thank author Tanya Lee Stone, who came in at the ninth hour to give me help on source notes and how to structure them when I was tearing my hair out in utter frustration.

I would also like to thank Ellen Slezak, Donna Rifkind, Denise Hamilton, Heather Dundas, Lienna Silver, Diane Arieff, Diana Wagman, and Amy Goldman Koss, who were my early readers; their support and friendship and stories have sustained me for years. I would also like to thank Nina Revyor and Sandy Jaffe, who provided resources and stories about their own experiences with *To Kill a Mockingbird*.

Finally, I want to thank my family . . . my sister, Keely, who came with me on the first trip, my husband, Kiffen, who came on the second trip, and my daughter Norah, who accompanied me the third time to Monroeville. I'm grateful for my daughter Lucy, a photographer, who looked at pictures with me for this book, and for my son, Flannery, who always listened and laughed when I called him up at college to tell him new stories and discoveries.

But most of all, I want to thank Nelle Harper Lee, who sat down and wrote a book over forty years ago.

Photo credits

P. 20: Monroe County Heritage Museums, Monroeville: The Search for Harper Lee's Maycomb

P. 29: Monroe County Heritage Museums Archives Collection

P. 31, left and right: Max McAliley Collection, Aaron White Photography. Special thanks to Monroe County Heritage Museums Archives Collection

P. 46: Monroe County Heritage Museums Archives Collection. Donated by Jennings Carter

P. 51: Max McAliley Collection, Aaron White Photography. Special thanks to Monroe County Heritage Museums Archives Collection

P. 64: The Associated Press

P. 69: Monroe County Heritage Museums Archives Collection

P. 77: Monroe County Heritage Museums Archives Collection

P. 84: 1947 Corolla (Vol. 55)/The University of Alabama

P. 97: The Associated Press

P. 117: The Associated Press

P. 122: New York World Telegram and the Sun Newspaper Photograph Collection (Library of Congress)

P. 136: Monroe County Heritage Museums Archives

P. 149: Max McAliley Collection, Aaron White Photography. Special thanks to Monroe County Heritage Museums Archives Collection

P. 160: The Associated Press